ARIZONA
Chimichangas

ARIZONA Chimichangas

RITA CONNELLY

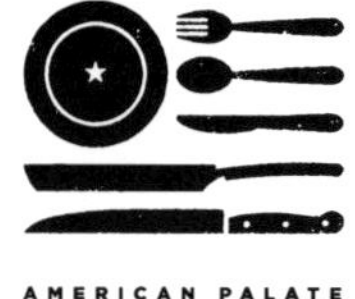

Published by American Palate
A Division of The History Press
Charleston, SC
www.historypress.com

Front cover image of large chimi courtesy of Macayo's. Back cover image of Cherry Chimi courtesy of Wisdom's Café, the La Piñata sign courtesy of La Piñata and all other images courtesy of the author.

First published 2019

Manufactured in the United States

ISBN 9781467140195

Library of Congress Control Number: 2018960962

Notice: The information in this book is true and complete to the best of our knowledge. It is offered without guarantee on the part of the author or The History Press. The author and The History Press disclaim all liability in connection with the use of this book.

To chimichanga lovers, wherever you may be,
and to my husband, John, for so many, many things.

CONTENTS

ACKNOWLEDGEMENTS

A big thank-you to all the people who helped make this task fun and tasty:

Carlotta Flores for everything.
Ken Lamberton for sharing his chimi search and his insight.
Ruben Soto for leading me to the Micha's Big Chimichanga celebration.
Juanita Reynoso and the team at Chalo's Casa Reynoso for food, stories and kindness and to all those people I called to get the family tree straight.
Karyn Zoldan and Edie Jarolim for their wit and wisdom.
Andi Berlin for her input, knowledge of Phoenix and outstanding driving skills.
Chef Gary Hickey from Charro Steak for his quick response to my questions about carne seca.
Roberta Reynoso and her girls on the phone at JR El Rey.
Andrea Esparza Sandoval for answering my countless questions about Globe-Miami food and for doing a little detective work on her own.
Karl De La Osa for the info on Yuma.
Luis Salazar and the team at St. Mary's Mexican Food for letting me watch the miracle of hand-making their famous tortillas.
Diane Hoopes at Casa Manana for her enthusiastic response (even though she wouldn't share her secret recipe for salsa).
Dr. Carlos G. Veléz-Ibañez for the invaluable information and delightful conversation.

Frank Gonzales III for his family's green chile recipe and for spreading Pancho's food to the rest of America (or at least West Virginia).

Alex Moreno Jr. for his family's stories about the "golden fried burrito."

Alex Franco for helping me dig out the details of Micha's giant chimi.

Marguerite Brown and Julie Valenzuela for all that great info about Al Valenzuela's legacy and the delicious mini-chimis.

Gilbert Molina III for telling me about his grandparents and their chimichanga story.

Tiffany Allison and Michele Woods for their enthusiastic sharing Aunt Chilada's stories.

Ashley Negron for her information and recipe from Macayo's.

Albert Vasquez from El Saguarito for his healthful take on Mexican fare.

Susan Timm at Knife & Fork Media Group.

Norma Gentry because she always has the answer.

Dave Fitzsimmons for his wit and opinions.

Gustavo Arellano, although we've never met, for his research and insight about Mexican foods.

Skip Jacob for the updates on the family's chimi stories.

Janice Vega of Havas PR for asking the right questions.

Matt Russell, Chris DiSimone, Bill Buckmaster, Adam Lehrman and Morning Blend KGUN 9 team for all their support.

Anthony Serrano for taking time to chat about the El Palacio Family's story and for sharing his recipe.

Demetri and Jeramya Wagner and their one-of-a-kind story and chimi.

Celeste Wisdom for answering all my questions.

Johnny Thoursavalas and Stefano Daniolos at Mi Patio for taking time from their busy schedules to chat.

Janie Riddle of Valle Luna for calling me back in a most timely manner (and for her friendly answers).

Leevon and Vincent Guerithault for letting me share the marvelous lobster chimi recipe and for your patience.

Fallon Kay for volunteering to get info for me even though we've never met in person.

John Gabaldon of Los Dos Molinos for answering my questions even though he was on vacation in Spain and for permission to use the adovada recipe.

Roxanne Samaniego of Casa Segovia for stories of her grandmother.

And, of course, the team at The History Press.

PROLOGUE

CHIMICHANGAS

SO MANY STORIES

What the cheesesteak is to Philadelphia and chicken wings are to Buffalo, the chimichanga is to the state of Arizona—the unofficial/official dish that represents the flavors, cultures and wonders found in the Grand Canyon State. This crispy dish is considered an Arizona original, and while stories as to its beginnings differ, what holds true is that there is nothing really like it anywhere. Another truth is that people have their favorite chimis from their favorite restaurants, and they will defend their choice down to the last bite. This book is an attempt to share their stories.

THE FIRST TIME

Unlike other foods I tried for the first time, I really don't remember my first taste of a chimichanga. Certainly, it was after I moved to Tucson in 1972. Back then, good Mexican food could only be found in southwestern states and California. I had heard of tacos and enchiladas and refried beans, but a deep-fried burro was not a part of my culinary vocabulary. When I say *burro*, I don't mean the animal. It is the term most Arizonans use to describe food wrapped in a flour tortilla. Other places use the word *burrito*. In this book, both terms will be used. Also, as a note, in the following pages "chili" means the meaty stew and "chile" means the pepper.

Once in Tucson, I fell immediately in love with Mexican food, specifically the Sonoran Mexican food found in Arizona. But as to when I ate my first chimi, I can't say. Obviously, I loved them, just like just about everyone else does. The crisp outside, the savory inside, the melted cheese on top—it all came together in the most wonderful way. And over the years (and during the writing of this book), I'll admit that I've had my fair share of them.

I learned that the chimichanga was supposedly created in Tucson (or Phoenix, depending on who you're talking with), and I learned that these delicious treats could be enhanced by topping them with enchilada sauce and more cheese and then put under the broiler for a few minutes. I learned they could be filled with just about anything, although at first the idea of dessert chimis seemed far-fetched.

I'm also not sure as to when the rest of America became familiar with chimichangas. But during my research, I found chimichangas on Mexican restaurant menus all over the United States. Diners can order chimis from Brooklyn to the Bay Area and from Traverse City to Tampa Bay. Check any school menu in just about any city in America and you'll see chimis served weekly. The freezer section at your grocery store has chimichangas, although in comparison to those found in restaurants, the quality may be in question. This culinary monster has traveled to the four corners of the earth.

There is a chain of restaurants in Great Britain called Chimichanga Tex-Mex that serves many a chimi. I also found an article online about Tucsonans eating chimis in Budapest. And should you be in Singapore and find yourself craving a chimi, no problem.

Telling the story of Arizona chimichangas reveals the stories of not just the people who created the dishes but also those who took a chance and followed a dream. These are stories of the families who worked hard to build a business and, in many cases, an empire. Some of the restaurants are relatively new; others have been around for decades and decades. Some are single standing places; others started that way but grew to two, three, six or ten sites. There are no chains included, but like Macayo and El Charro, several restaurants have multiple sites often in more than one city.

As an aside, the stories are told, for the most part, by the people who are the center of each story (or at least a family member or former employee) and thus are told how they remember people, places and events. Whether their memories are exactly how events actually played out doesn't matter. The stories are the memories; the memories are the stories.

The arrangement of the book grew organically. At first, I'd planned to divide the state into northern, southern, eastern and western Arizona quadrants, and while I retained that pattern somewhat, as I did my research, I discovered that certain culinary pockets are found throughout the state.

The Globe-Miami area is a prime example. With dozens of Mexican restaurants located in this area, which was once a thriving mining community, the food here has distinct flavors and styles. Add the fact that most of the Mexican restaurants in the area are owned by generations of the same family and the circle is full.

Another distinct culinary pocket is the "Salsa Trail." The Salsa Trail is in the Gila River area and is spread through three different counties: Graham, Cochise and Greenlee. The flavors are decidedly different with touches from neighboring New Mexico.

Tucson and Phoenix each deserve their own chapters, not just because of the high concentrations of restaurants but because they both lay claim to the origins of the chimichanga. On the other hand, the farther north you go, the farther you get away from the Sonoran region and fewer chimis are found, although it seems the chimis choices are more creative.

By Sonoran region, I mean the geographic area that lies between 100 to 150 miles on either side of the Mexican border. Influences are abundant in food, drink, décor, dress and daily living. Granted, the American side of the border is what this book is all about; nevertheless, the decades of being a part of Mexico has shaped the way things are done in this culturally rich part of the state.

Chimis are a must on menus in Phoenix, Tucson and just about every other city or town in the state. Just about every Mexican restaurant in Arizona has chimichangas on their menus, with most places using the same fillings: red chili, green chili, shredded beef of some kind, chicken, beans and rice.

There are a few original and offbeat versions, which will be explored in later pages. But a chimi is a chimi, right? In truth, the differences come from the people who make the chimis. A red chili in Safford is different from a red chili in Tucson or Sedona or Yuma. Chicken is prepared in many different ways, from simple pulled chicken to smoked chicken to grilled. Even simple refried beans taste different depending on who's stirring the pot.

Some of the recipes are decades old, handed down from generation to generation. Some take flavors from other cultures. Some are bold attempts to elevate the dish. Ingredients differ. The tortillas, the chiles and the preparation of the meats can hold local flavors (this is especially true of chiles that are influenced by the soil and water used much in the way grapes reflect their terroir). So, even though you order a green chili chimichanga every time you eat at a Mexican restaurant, you will taste different flavors thanks to personal touches and family secrets.

Time and distance made it impossible to eat every chimichanga in the book, so for those I couldn't get to I relied on recommendations from friends who lived near the restaurants and food writers from other publications. I researched in local newspapers. I spoke with restaurant owners, managers and chefs whose passion for their work was inspiring. I looked for chimis that weren't run of the mill—the ones that were topped with something besides enchilada sauce. But fear not—plenty of the traditional favorites are included.

A term arose that did stump me (and just about everyone I talked to) was "wet chimis." We deduced that meant enchilada style where after a trip to the fryer a chimi is covered with enchilada sauce, cheese and then popped under the broiler for just a bit, but "wet" is not a term we use in Arizona. The Internet revealed that the term is common in California, Michigan, Utah, Washington State and a few other places. In Colorado and New Mexico, they use the term "smothered."

People did suggest topping chimis with a fried egg. A cream sauce was also a favorite, but even those sauces vary from kitchen to kitchen. Additions to the sauces include jalapeño peppers, poblano peppers, cilantro, lime, horseradish and many others.

There were other serving suggestions as well, but not all toppings met with success, the exception being that fried egg. One person told about ordering a chimi at a national chain—not in Arizona—and the restaurant smothered the chimi with *beef gravy*, an absolute taboo as far as chimi aficionados are concerned. Another person told about how a restaurant used tomato sauce from a can. And there have been numerous reports of mayonnaise being slavered over the top—more about that odd topping later.

This book will explore the controversial history of chimis, including the various and many claims to the origin. More than a few restaurants swear that they created the chimichanga. Others say that chimis crossed the border with Chinese immigrants when Mexico expelled the Chinese. Some folks believe that the first chimis come from a little town in Mexico, where they're called "chivichangas."

Diana Kennedy, the queen bee of authentic Mexican food, wrote that chimichangas were served deep into Mexico for decades, although she called them "chivichangas" too (a point that will be discussed later). Still others remember sampling a version at the Yaqui Indian Reservation near Tucson.

All these stories are fun, clever and believable and will be explored in this book. It should be noted that in spite of all the claims, there is a deep respect among all the restaurateurs for one another.

I've also included a trip to a tortilla factory where the big flour tortillas are made, complete with photos.

Speaking of recipes, I've included several recipes so people can make chimis at home. The recipes were gleaned from the restaurant owners and their families. But restaurants like to keep recipes secret, so some of the recipes are from home cooks or chef friends. You'll find recipes for fillings, salsas and toppings and an explanation on how to make a proper chimi. There is also a glossary of Mexican foods.

I've included the addresses of all the restaurants mentioned in this book in case anyone wants to take a chimi tour of Arizona. Should you decide to make a chimichanga pilgrimage, the only recommendations are to take your time so that you can enjoy the beauty and the other outstanding amenities the state has to offer and to loosen your belts (better yet, don't wear one).

TALES OF THE CHIMICHANGA

It's a debatable thing, like politics, only you don't get offended.
—Carlotta Flores, interview, December 2017

I don't know which of these might be the truth....I'd honestly rather eat the things than argue about their origins.
—Dr. James Griffith, from Tucson's Mexican Restaurants: Repasts, Recipes and Remembrances

El Charro

Monica Flin opened El Charro in 1922, and in spite of relocating a few times, having bad years, battling the IRS and being a single woman in a time when women didn't own businesses, Flin found great success.

But "Tia Monica," as everyone called her, was always a little bit ahead of her time. Her grandniece, Carlotta Flores, the current owner and chef of El Charro, has a book full of stories about Tia Monica.

Flin was the eldest child of eight. Her father, Jules Flin, a sculptor from France, had been commissioned to create the entrance to the new cathedral in Tucson. Jules Flin also built a family home that Monica turned into El Charro about the same time the chimi event happened.

Monica hunted and fished, she took her nieces and nephews to Los Angeles for shopping sprees by train and she hosted card parties for the

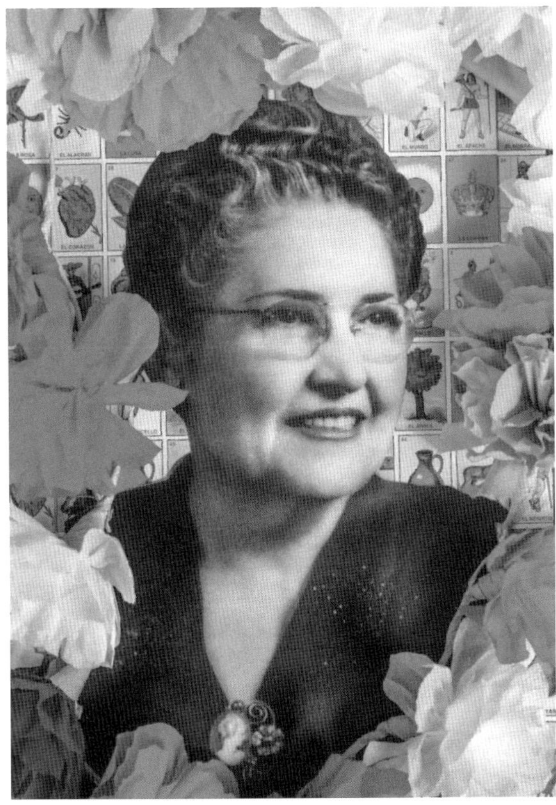

Left: Tia Monica. *Courtesy of El Charro.*

Below: El Charro's famous chimichanga. *Author photo.*

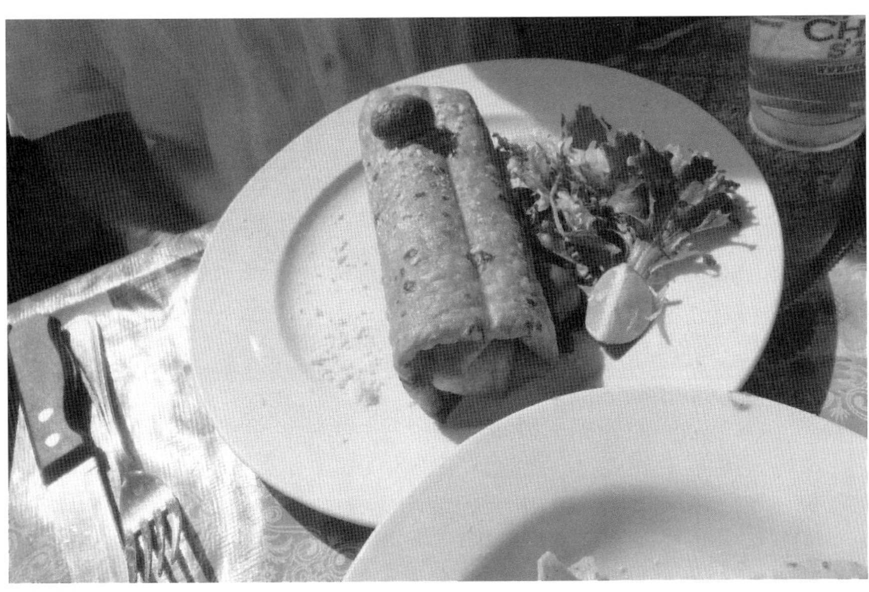

neighborhood women where the tea was spiked with tequila or whiskey (during Prohibition, no less). Flin traveled often. She had a romantic love life and even married for a short while. She was known to have a very colorful vocabulary.

It's not hard to imagine the night in her kitchen when the chimichanga was supposed to have been created. Kids were underfoot. Everyone was hungry. The stove was filled with boiling pots. Then, accidently, Tia Monica dropped a burro in the hot oil, as chefs are known to do. Flin started to shout a Mexican curse word that sounded similar to chimichanga, but in deference to the children, she quickly changed it to "chimichanga," which depending on who you talk to means "thingamajig," "trinket" or absolutely nothing.

Now, being a practical businesswoman, Flin would never throw out perfectly good, albeit overcooked, food, so she tried it, liked it and knew others would like it, too. Carlotta thinks she may have been there among all the kids because her own mother was, and she testified to seeing and hearing the whole thing.

Today, El Charro is America's oldest Mexican restaurant run by the same family. People flock to the downtown El Charro spot (one of several in Tucson), and there's a waiting line on most evenings. They come for the enchiladas, tacos, tamales and, of course, the chimichangas.

Made with eighteen-inch-diameter locally made tortillas, the chimis at El Charro are legendary. Fillings include red or green chili, chicken prepped numerous and tasty ways, refried beans, grilled vegetables (there is even a gluten-free tortilla) and El Charro's famous carne seca. El Charro makes its carne seca from a cut called a wedge from just off the rib. It is pounded thin, seasoned and then dried in the hot Arizona sun—like jerky but more flavorful.

The 1997 Sunset Mexican Cookbook calls chimichangas "Sonoran tacos."

El Charro uses large cages that were created just for the purpose of drying the carne seca. Two large cages are kept on the roof. Once it is perfectly dried, the meat is then mixed with chiles, tomatoes, onions and spices and heated quickly on the flattop. The mixture is moist, smoky and almost sweet. Jane and Michael Stern, in their book *Road Food*, wax poetic about the carne seca: "It's like the meat blossomed. Once you've had it, mere ground beef will never satisfy again." The Sterns think so much of Carlotta's food that they co-wrote a cookbook with Carlotta, *El Charro Café Cookbook: Flavors of Tucson from America's Oldest Family-Operated Mexican Restaurant.*

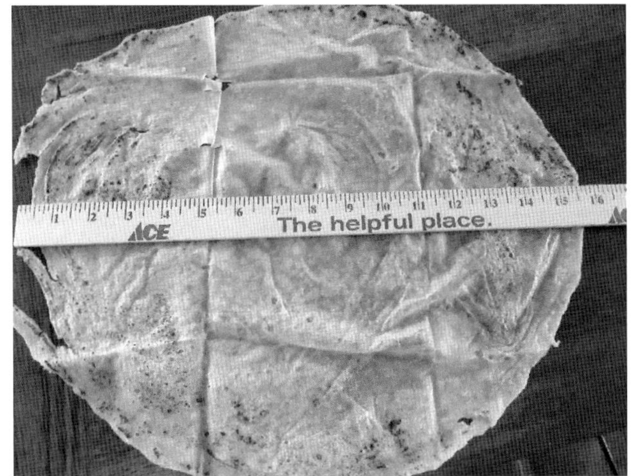

Sixteen inches of flavor. *Author photo.*

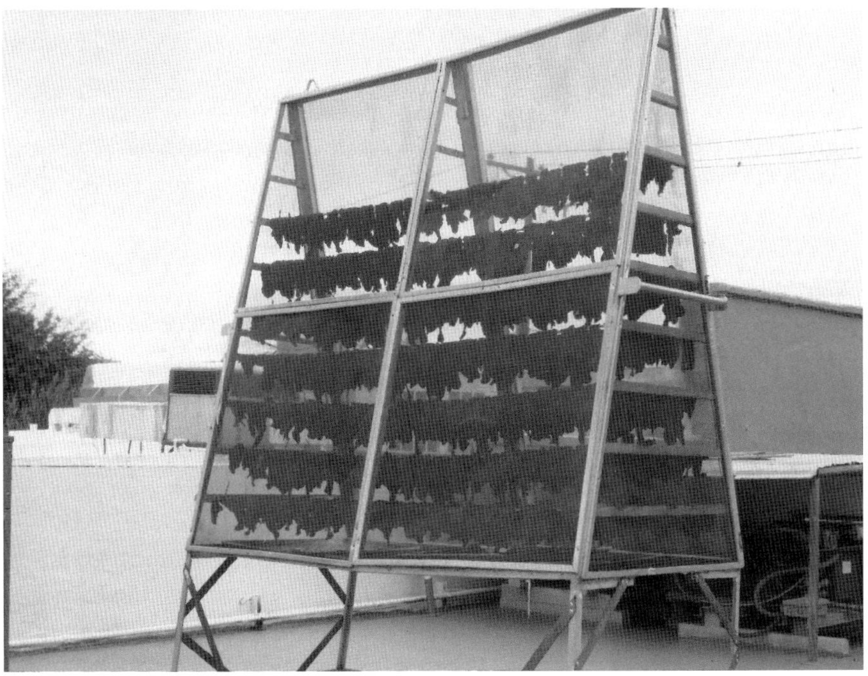

The carne seca cage is lifted to the roof at El Charro. *Author photo.*

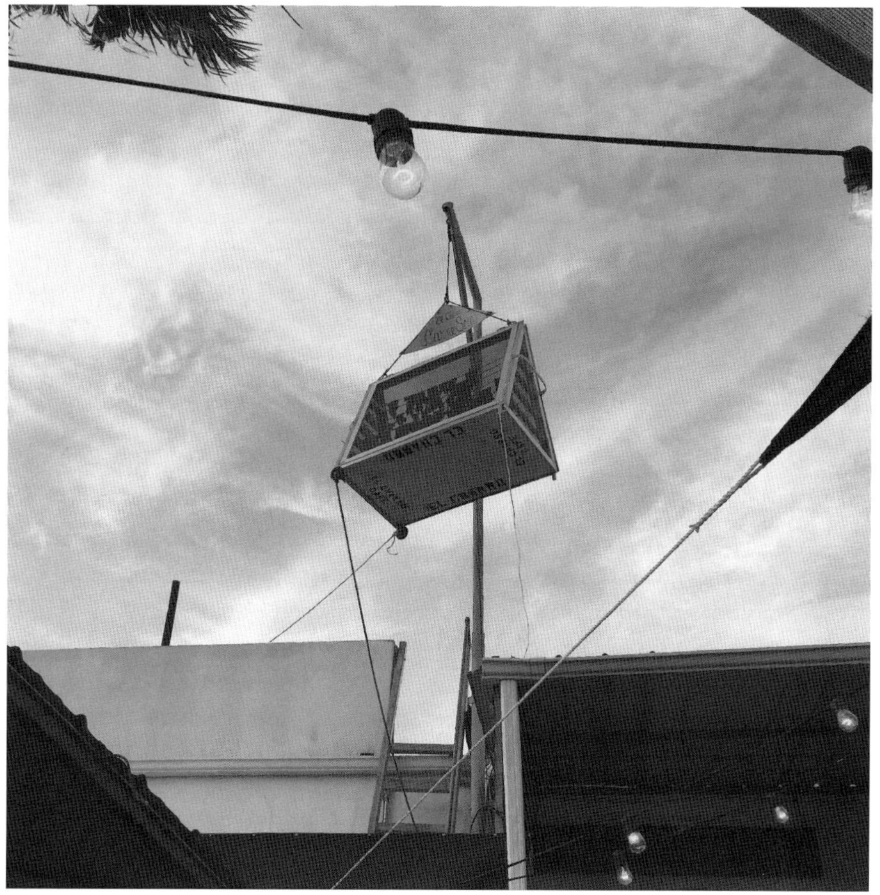

Up and away, the carne seca drying cage on the way to the roof at El Charro. *Author photo.*

El Charro sells thousands of chimis per week. *USA Today* sang the praises of the chimis at El Charro, calling them "some of the biggest and best" and called the carne seca one of the best plates in America. Inspired by such high praise, Carlotta created a special chimi just for the daily, calling it the USA Today Chimichanga. Larger than normal, it was filled with carne seca, beans, cheese, rice, guacamole, sour cream and salsa.

In 2008, *Gourmet* named El Charro one of "America's Legendary Restaurants."

Besides the main restaurant located in a historic district just north of downtown, Flores and her family operate two other El Charros in Tucson; a more casual concept, Sir Veza's, in Tucson and in airports in Phoenix,

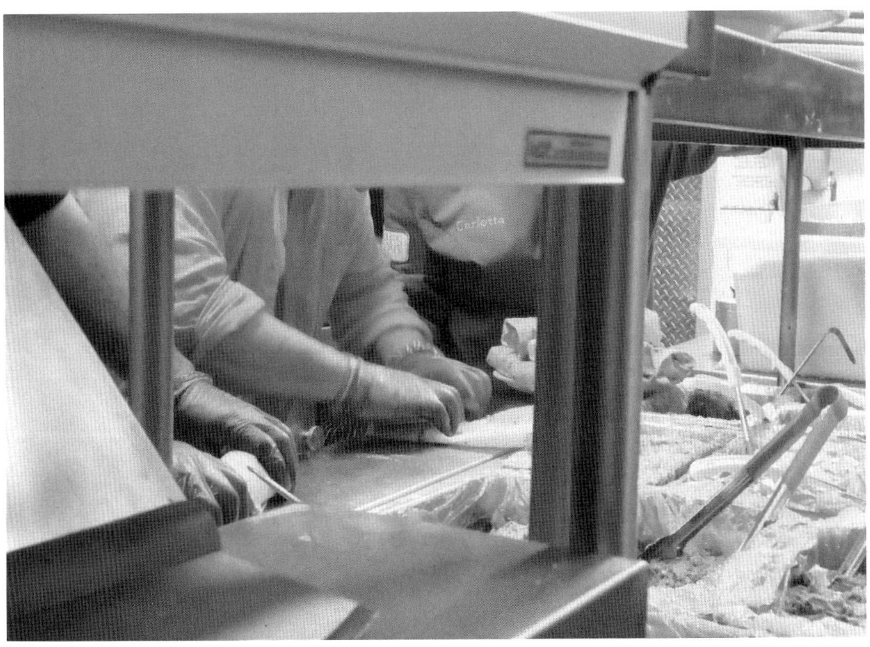

Rolling chimis at El Charro. *Author photo.*

Tucson and even Baltimore; and a third concept, Hecho in Vegas, at the MGM Grand in Las Vegas.

Remarkably, there is even an El Charro Under the Sea, located on the USS *Tucson* submarine. There is also a large catering outlet and Carlotta's Kitchen, which makes and sells salsas and other condiments used in the restaurants. Order El Charro's great food at www.carlottaskitchen.com.

Macayo's

The Macayo chimi story is similar to that of El Charro in that the whole thing was just an accident. Woody Johnson, a well-known lover of burros and a relatively new restaurant owner, was in the kitchen one night making himself a burro when he accidently dropped his dinner in the deep-fryer. Voila! A chimi was born, and Johnson decided to put it on the menu at his tiny restaurant, El Nido.

Woody Johnson and his wife, Victoria, had little if any restaurant experience when they opened their place in 1946. Using Woody's family's delicious recipes, their tiny restaurant had a mere six tables and served one hundred diners per week.

The place was always packed, and soon they realized that they needed to grow. In 1952, they opened a new spot on Central Avenue in Phoenix and named it Woody's Macayo, which would become the first of a restaurant empire that spanned multiple cities and two states.

Woody and Victoria grew up in Superior, a mining town about seventy miles east of Phoenix. Vicky's parents were Lebanese, and Woody's mom was from Mexico; his dad was a miner who had emigrated through Mexico from Sweden.

The two were childhood sweethearts and married on Christmas Eve 1940. He'd worked at the mines, which he knew wasn't the way he wanted to go, but then World War II began and Woody enlisted in the U.S. Navy in 1943. He wanted to be a pilot, but his poor eyesight quashed those plans, yet he served his country with honor.

Upon his return home, he took a job at AirResearch Manufacturing. There he learned the best techniques for managing a line and people, a talent that would go a long way to his future success, although he didn't know that at the time.

But Woody's life was a series of plans not always going the way he thought they might, although in the long run everything turned out for the best for him, for his family and for the entire valley. And it all began because he was hungry and decided to check out his brother-in-law George Romley's new restaurant, Valle de Sol.

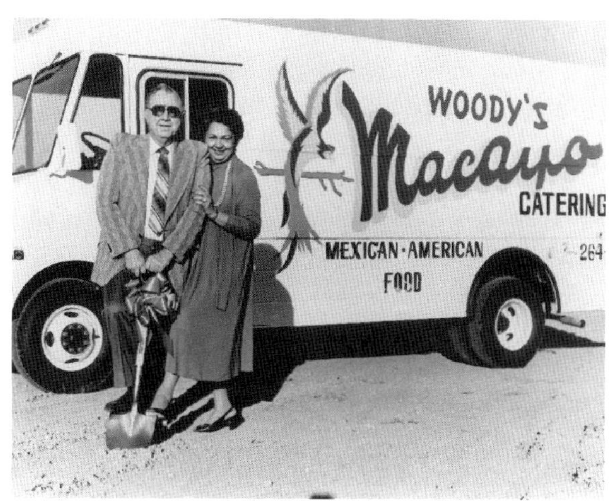

The truck from Macayo's.
Courtesy of Macayo's.

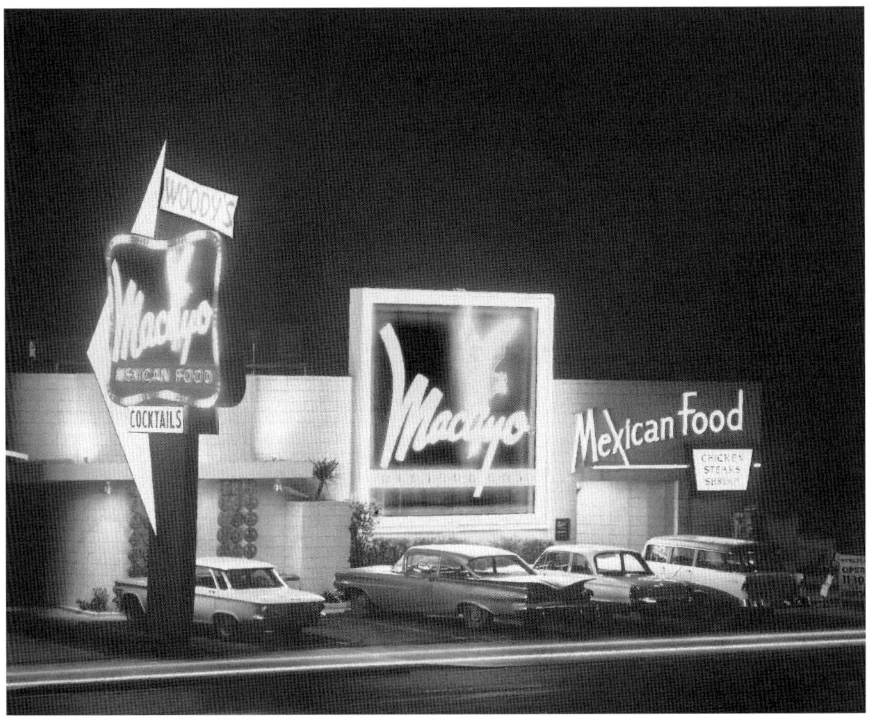

Macayo's at night. *Courtesy of Macayo's.*

He walked into a scene of chaos. Woody stepped up to the plate, so to speak, and volunteered to help using the techniques he'd learned at AirReseach. The line in the kitchen was soon running like a well-oiled machine, and Woody was offered a part of the business.

Shortly thereafter, he and Victoria opened Woody's Dining Room on Central Avenue, which at the time was so remote that parts of Central Avenue were still dirt. The closest neighbors were a dance hall and a dairy farm.

Business was good, but Vicky hung on to her job at a bank to ensure a steady income. She worked at the restaurant in the evenings. People loved the place. The food was homemade and the service friendly. A charming touch, which today seems impossible, was how a parrot and a donkey greeted guests at the door. Woody was known to give kids rides on the donkey. This stopped at the request of the health department, but that didn't stop the crowds.

In 1949, the Johnsons moved their restaurants to McDowell Road and, in 1953, renamed the business Woody's El Macayo, perhaps as a tribute to the retired bird (Macayo means "macaw" in Spanish). Until 1959, Romley was still a part of the business, as an ad in the October 21 edition of the *Arizona Republic* announced that the Johnsons had bought out Romley. That was the same year that a Macayo's opened in Las Vegas.

The business began to expand. Year by year, decade by decade, the Macayo empire grew to seventeen restaurants statewide. Today, there are eight—six in the Phoenix area and two in Las Vegas.

Eventually, the business expanded into catering and a cannery, which produced many of the Macayo products. When access to quantities of good chiles became difficult, the Johnsons started their own chile farm in Douglas in southeastern Arizona.

Of course, the chimichanga is an integral part of the Macayo legend. For a time, the company held a fundraiser called Chimi Fest. Special chimis were created. Grandson Bubba created the Bubba-Q chimi that was stuffed with his secret pork recipe. A granddaughter created the chicken poblano chimi where a chicken-filled chile is wrapped in the tortilla before being dropped in the fryer. Macayo's donated a portion of the money to various charities in the Valley. Giving back to the community has always been central to the Macayo philosophy.

And while the menu lists plenty of chimis, a new twist was added recently called "Gimme a Chimi." Customers can build their own chimis. First, they pick a protein (shredded beef, shredded chicken, chalupa, pork carnitas and red or green chile pork stew). Then they add a sauce (relleno sauce or fire-roasted tomatillo sauce) and then a topping (sour cream, guacamole or Baja sauce) and finally a side of beans or rice.

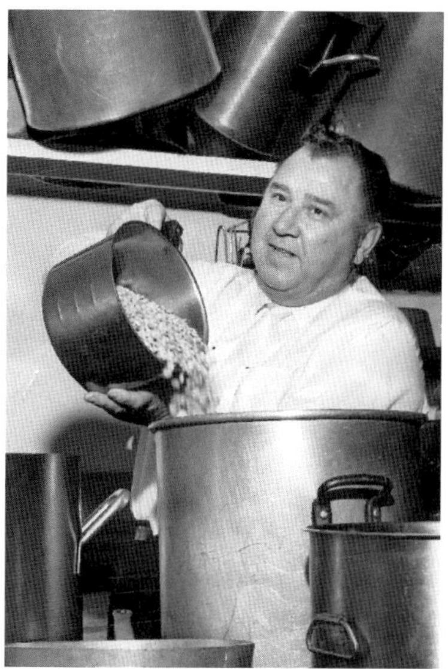

Woody in the kitchen. *Courtesy of Macayo's.*

In 2011, a record was broken thanks to Woody and Macayo: "Most People to Share a Chimi." Held at the Changing Hands Bookstore, fifteen people shared one chimi (check it out on recordsetters.com).

Woody was also the impetus behind trying to get the chimichanga to be named the official food of Arizona. He, along with Carlotta Flores of El Charro and a handful of other restaurateurs, made the proposal to no avail. The legislature apparently had more serious things on the agenda.

Woody was a major player in the business until just before his death in 1999. Vicky died in 2011.

The three Johnson children, and their children, are now in charge of the various entities of the business. Daughter Sharisse is CEO. Son Gary is president, and another son, Stephan, is partner and board member. Daughter-in-law Nana is in charge of the interior decoration. Various grandchildren work a full spectrum of jobs.

The newest entity, Woody's Macayo, opened in 2017. Certainly bigger than the tiny six-table original restaurant, it is a little flashier but still holds the same vibe. From the refurbished tables and chairs to the large mural on the wall, the newest Macayo's is an homage to Woody and Victoria.

And while a few new additions have been made to the menu, diners can still find Woody's enchiladas, tacos, tamales and, of course, his world-famous chimichangas.

Club 21

Club 21 is one of Tucson's oldest Mexican restaurants run by the same family (and in the same location). George Jacob opened his place in 1946 with his brothers, who eventually went on to other things.

Located smack dab in the middle of Tucson's Miracle Mile, a major route to Phoenix where dozens of motor hotels were filled with thousands of tourists, Club 21 met with instant success. The restaurant was expanded over time, and today the place is run by George's son, Skip, and grandson, Taft Jr.

As the Club 21 story goes, one night one of those tourists from "Back East" ordered a burro and, not understanding what a flour tortilla was, raised a ruckus claiming that his dinner was not "cooked." George took the burro back to the kitchen and tossed it on the griddle with some oil, turning the tortilla a golden brown. The diner was so pleased that George decided to put the fried burro on the menu.

Later, when another customer commented on the dish saying "que changa" ("how clever") the name caught on, eventually morphing into "chimichanga."

At one point in time, George wanted to write a book about chimis but never got the chance. He died in 2005. Skip noted that the story is true but also that they served fried burros on request.

MI RANCHITO

From an interview with Alex Moreno Jr., January 2018

Mi Ranchito's chimichanga story is one of necessity being the mother of invention. Alex Moreno recalled that as a child he and his two brothers were raised by their grandparents in Tucson. Their father, Alex Moreno Sr., had run a kitchen as part of the bracero program during World War II in Tucson.

Due to agriculture labor shortage during the war, the State Department along with the Department of Labor and Immigration and Naturalization Services brought laborers from Mexico (and Guam) to fill the positions needed. They were promised a thirty-cent-per-hour wage, decent housing, sanitation and food. Alex Sr. cooked for the braceros, and when the war ended, he decided to open a restaurant. He also bought himself a brand-new 1946 Chevrolet (keep that date in mind).

The restaurant, Mi Ranchito, was in the tiny farm community of Avondale, just west of Phoenix. Alex Sr. would travel to Tucson to visit his boys every other week. The drive at that time was a long one, up to six hours, as the freeway system was nonexistent in Arizona. His mother, concerned that her son would get hungry on the long drive home, always prepared a stack of burros to eat along the way.

In 1982, after a redistricting of parts of southern Arizona, Senator Mo Udall had to choose which one he wanted to represent. He chose the one with the best chimichangas.

One night, he returned to the restaurant with the burros still intact. He was hungry, but his wife, Rosa, told him she had just shut down the kitchen; the only thing still available was the deep-fryer. They decided to fry the burros but were concerned that they would fall apart in the fryer, so they stuck a few toothpicks in the burro to secure it. What came out of the fryer was a crispy, golden treat.

At about that same time, there was a customer who came into the restaurant every day for every meal, breakfast, lunch and dinner. He asked Alex and Rosa if there was anything different that he could have. As Alex Jr. explained it, his dad and Rosa decided to make him one of their creations. They called it a "golden-fried burrito." Who could pass up something with a name like that?

The man was amazed by the new treat. He told everyone he knew about the golden fried burrito, and since Avondale was the kind of place where everyone knew everyone else, other people started asking for the item. It became a permanent part of the menu.

When the Morenos closed Mi Ranchito and opened another restaurant in Phoenix called La Rosa, they brought their creation with them. Alex Jr. said that no one else in the Phoenix area was serving anything like it, not even Macayo.

Eventually, La Rosa closed when Rosa got cancer. By this time, the Moreno boys were grown, and Alex Jr. opened a restaurant in Tucson called Don Jose's. He said they didn't serve the golden fried burrito there because it was more of a fast-food place and frying a burro properly takes too long.

At one point, a customer came in and asked for a chimichanga. Moreno had no idea what he was talking about and decided to do a little detective work around town, where he found his father's golden fried burrito being served at several restaurants in Tucson. He couldn't really do anything about it, but his ads in the Tucson newspapers noted that the Don Jose's was run by the Moreno family, who were the first people to put chimis on the menu.

Another origin story is one of practicality. Luis Salazar from St. Mary's Mexican Food in Tucson recalled his grandmother telling him that chimis originated in the fields of Mexico. Workers usually had little time to eat and needed a hand-held food that ate like a sandwich. Burros worked great but were messy, so wives would pan-fry their husbands' meals in a little lard and flip them over, and although they weren't called "chimichangas," they were still "fried burros."

The fact that Alex Sr.'s car was a 1946 model puts a timeline on their discovery, and since other stories don't have that specific of a date for when they put their chimis on the menu, there may be some credence to the fact that Alex and Rosa Moreno were the originators of chimichangas.

CASA MOLINA

Another story takes the origin of the chimichanga to Nogales, Sonora, Mexico, the border twin town to Nogales, Arizona. Elias Molina, of the

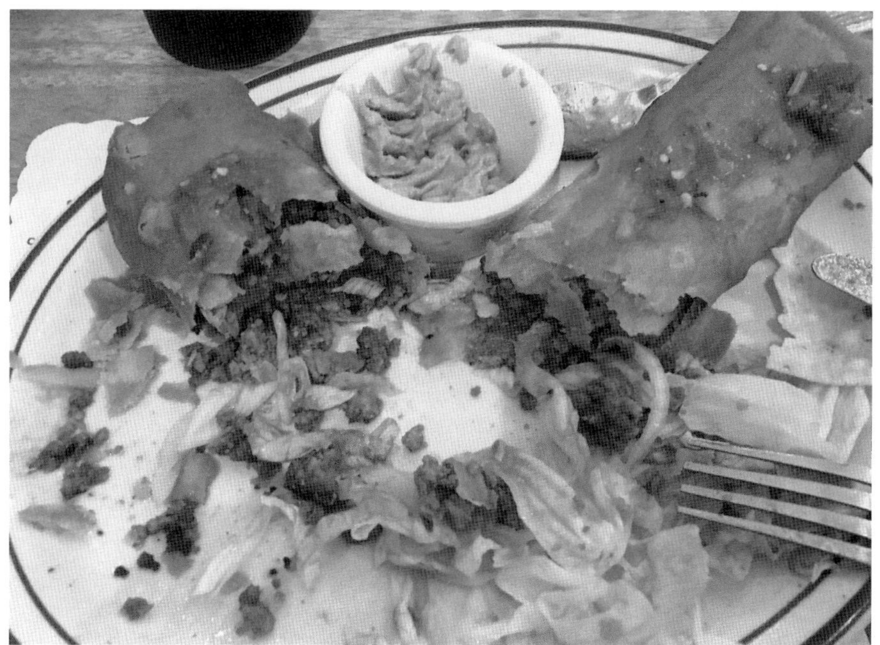

A red chili chimi from Casa Molina. *Author photo.*

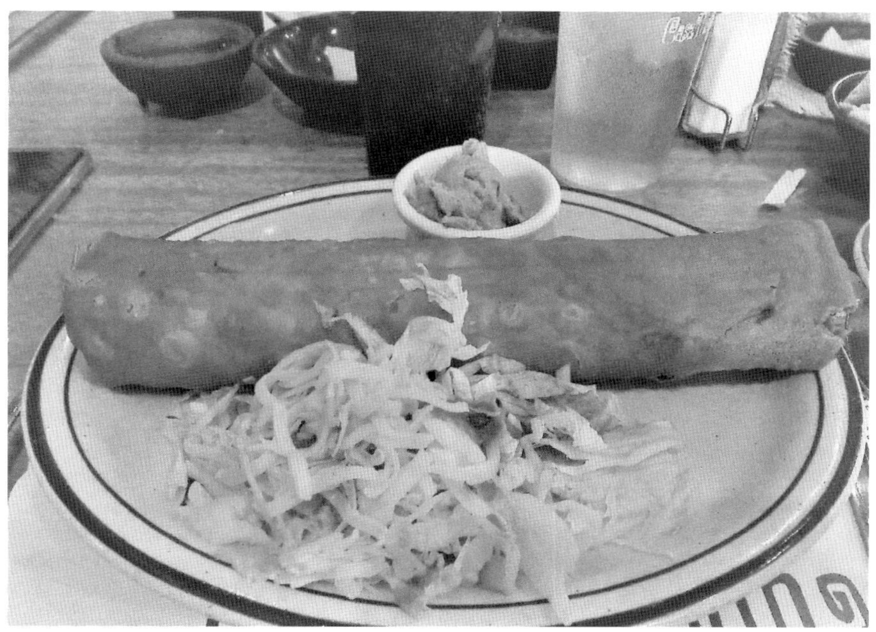

Casa Molina's chimis are long, narrow and crispy. *Author photo.*

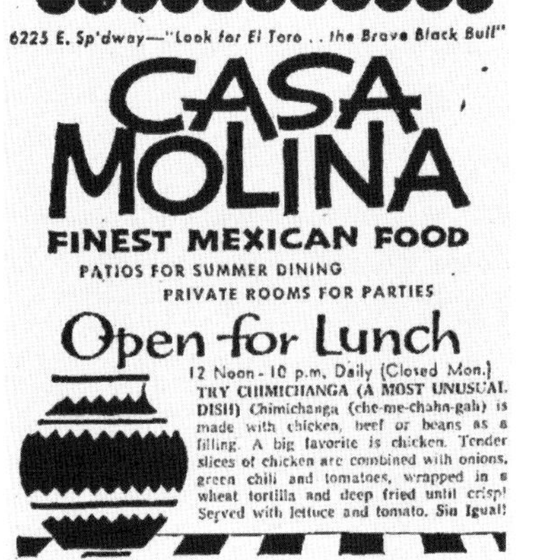

Ad from the 1961 *Arizona Daily Star*.

famed Molina family restaurant empire, swears that his father, Gilberto, often visited a bar there called La Frontera. There, the owner's wife, by the name of Lucy Meza, an Indian woman, would feed her baby burros, but when she accidentally dropped one in hot oil, she decided to give it to her child despite the error. Elias added that she called her creation "chimichanga," which means "papoose" or "doll" in her native tongue.

The Molina family has had restaurants in Tucson since the 1950s, and the chimis they serve look decidedly different than most other chimis. At Casa Molina (one of several Molina restaurants), the chimis are as long as your plate, thin and unbelievably crispy, which is similar to the way Gilberto saw them in Nogales.

In an early article in the *Tucson Citizen*, Elias Molina noted the Molina family was the first to put chimis on a menu. His grandson backed the claim. Early menus aren't available, but this story has been repeated over the decades as part of the Molina family lore.

THE CHINESE CONNECTION

There is speculation in some quarters that chimis aren't Mexican at all but rather a creation by Chinese cooks in Mexico sometime around the turn of the twentieth century.

Hundreds of Chinese immigrated to the Sonoran region in the late 1800s and early 1900s. According to the theory, Mexican men married Chinese women, who cooked egg rolls and other foods of their country for their spouses but used the ingredients available (i.e., flour tortillas).

Time-wise, the numbers don't quite add up, and the majority of émigrés were men who worked on farms in Mexico and on the railroad in the United States. They would leave their families behind, working with the hopes of bringing the families to America. That took years. Some married Mexican women, so perhaps it was the Mexican wives who in trying to make egg rolls for their husbands created the chimichanga.

GORDO'S

Gordo's Mexicateria and Mexicatessen's chimi origin story is a simple one. A customer came into the restaurant a short time after it opened in 1959 and wondered if the owner, Diego "Al" Valenzuela, could make a fried burrito. Never one to say no to a customer, Valenzuela plopped a burro into the fryer, and the rest, as they say, is chimichanga history. While not many people are as aware of this story as some of the others, it should be noted that Valenzuela was undoubtedly the person who made chimichangas a household word in Tucson at least.

Valenzuela had been a highly successful insurance salesman. He considered a political career for a while, but then he decided that he wanted to open a restaurant that would serve the food he grew up eating. The original restaurant was tiny and located on what was then the northwest side of Tucson. Food was served cafeteria style because, as daughter Marguerite Brown noted in an interview a few years back, her dad didn't like waiting for his food and didn't want his customers to wait either. He wanted them to feel like they were in their grandmother's kitchen, where they could just fill a plate of great food hot off the stove.

Over time, the restaurant was relocated to the eastside of Tucson; at one time, the family ran two restaurants. Chimis of all sorts were always served. Green chili, red chili, ground beef, refried beans and chicken chimis attracted a large following.

Then, sometime in the early 1980s, Valenzuela realized that he needed to expand his marketing beyond a few radio and newspaper ads, so he began a series of television ads that changed everything.

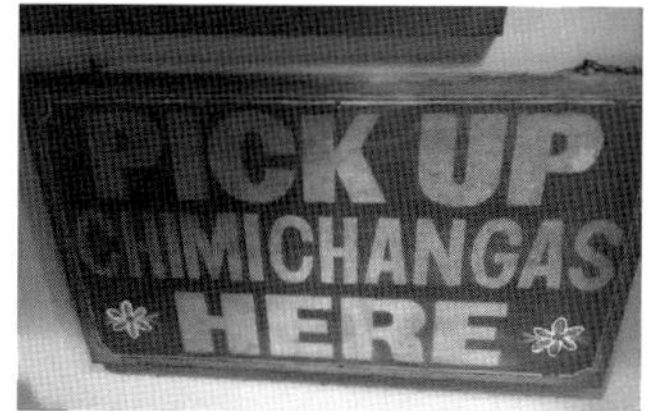

Get your chimi that-away. *Courtesy of the Valenzuela family.*

Valenzuela wasn't sure that he was the best person to appear in the ads. Wife Julie remembered hearing her husband practice in the shower, but according to Brown, her dad was a natural spokesperson. Valenzuela was acutely aware of two basic tenants of advertising: leave customers knowing who you are and make sure they know what you're selling. With that in mind, he struck on the catchphrase that would become a part of Tucson culinary history.

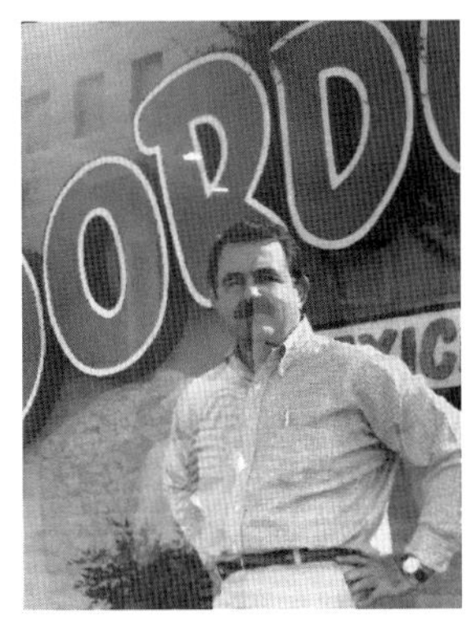

Diego Valenzuela. "If you like chimichangas…." *Courtesy of the Valenzuela family.*

Today, there is hardly a Tucsonan of a certain age who, when you mention Gordo's, doesn't reply with the words, "Do you like chimichangas? I mean, do you *reeeally* like chimichangas? Then come on down to Gordo's." The reaction is almost Pavlovian and always said with a huge smile.

The ads varied a little over the years, but Valenzuela appeared in all of them. Sometimes he was in front of the restaurant; sometimes there was just a simple black background. Valenzuela emphasized the quality of the ingredients, the quantity of the servings, the cleanliness of the restaurant and, of course, the chimichangas.

In one ad, he noted that Tucson is the Mexican food capital of the United States; in another, he claimed the city to be the chimichanga capital of the United States. Sometimes he wore a cowboy hat, but he always wore a white shirt and tie.

In 1986, Gordo's chimis were named "Best in Tucson" by the *Arizona Daily Star*, which was soon added to the ads.

Gordo's sold more than 150 chimis per day. The demand was so great that a commissary was built to speed up production. Products were sold at Costco and Fry's grocery stores. Valenzuela was dubbed the "Chimichanga King" by locals.

People remember the homey atmosphere, the free guacamole and sour cream served at each table, the chocolate mints at the end of every meal and Valenzuela's "commanding presence." Gordo's was the kind of place where people headed straight from the airport; the kind of place they brought out-of-town

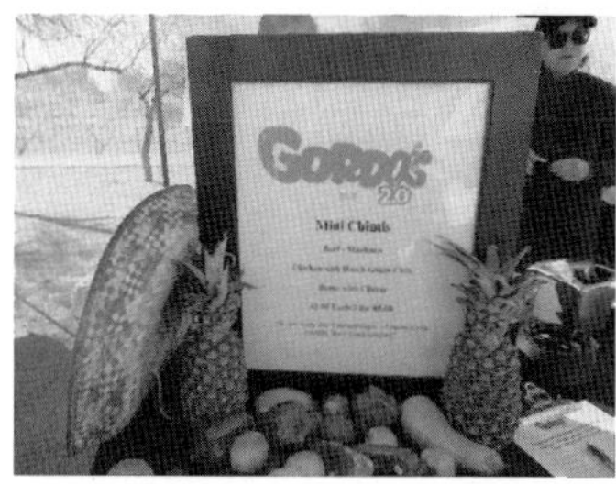

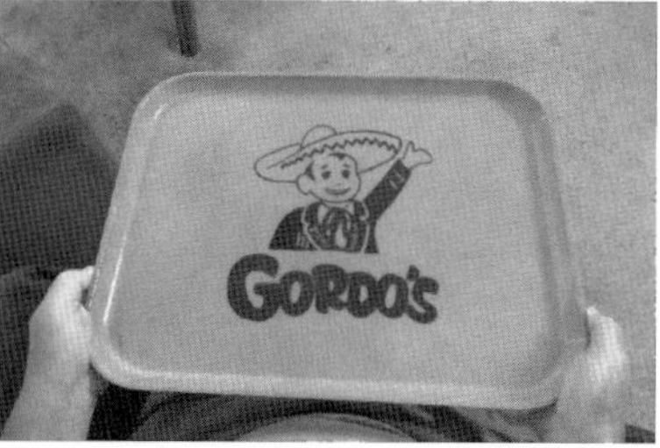

Left: Yum! Gordo's 2.0. *Right*: A tray from the original Gordo's Mexicateria and Mexicatessen. *From the author's collection.*

guests. It was family-friendly with family-friendly prices, like $1.99 for a chimi with rice or beans. At lunch and dinner, tables were filled with parents, kids, grandparents, cousins, aunts and uncles. Businesspeople, government types and students all ate at Gordo's.

Valenzuela was known for his generosity to the community and his love for palomino horses. He worked every day until the day he sold the restaurant in 2000 after forty-five years in business. He spent retirement with his family, continuing his community support and raising his beloved palominos.

Al Valenzuela died in 2003, leaving behind a legacy of good food and the catchphrase that defines Tucson and its love for the fried burro: "If you like chimichangas. I mean if you *reeeally* like chimichangas…." The ads can be viewed on YouTube.

Recently, daughter Marguerite Brown decided to bring back her dad's chimis. Instead of opening a restaurant, she and her partner, Mark Callahan, along with mom Julie Valenzuela, sell mini-chimis at local farmers' markets. They call their venture Gordo's 2.0. Marguerite charms the crowds, and Mark makes the chimis in a tiny deep-fryer as people order them. Julie quietly supervises. They come in three flavors: machaca, chicken and bean and cheese. Topped with Gordo's salsa and an artful squiggle of crema, the chimis are hot and crispy and bring back all those wonderful food memories of Gordo's.

In Tucson's Barrio in 1900, the Chinese population was 177 men and 7 women. By 1910, the numbers had boomed to 224. Farm workers in Mexico never exceeded 200 people. General Pershing had 375 Chinese who traveled with him as he chased Pancho Villa into Mexico. They worked as merchants, launderers and cooks. Perhaps these cooks created the first chimis.

The number of Chinese was relatively small because there were numerous immigration laws that severely restricted—and for a while prohibited—Chinese and other "foreigners" from entering the United States. Laborers weren't allowed; one had to be of a higher class to be allowed in the United States. If you were a teacher, a student, a merchant or a diplomat, or just passing through, you were considered worthy, yet even these groups found hatred and bigotry rampant in most of America.

In 1988, the Arizona Daily Star reported that a Montana moose chimichanga came in third place at the Wild Game Cook-Off in Tucson.

In Mexico, life wasn't much better. The Mexican Revolution resulted in more than one thousand Chinese being expelled from the country. On May 15, 1911, half the Chinese population in Torreon, Coahulia (three hundred) was slaughtered by revolutionary troops.

Many moved to southern Arizona, where they became truck farmers, opened neighborhood markets and worked in the few restaurants. Again, here was another opportunity to blend culinary cultures, but there is no proof that anything like that happened. None of that adds up to chimichangas being created by the Chinese.

SIMULTANEOUS COMBUSTION

Dr. Carlos G. Vélez-Ibañez, Regents' Professor at Arizona State University, was raised in Tucson and said, "As a kid, in probably the late '40s or early '50s, I had a chimichanga at the old El Charro [downtown off Congress Street], which predates Macayo." But he added, "I have an inkling that chimis were also being made in Nogales at about the same time." He also believes that the Tohono O'odham, one of the Native American people in the area, made some version of chimichangas. He called it "simultaniosicity," the idea that certain items evolved at the same time in different places.

Whatever the truth, Dr. Veléz-Ibañez said that chimichangas are most definitely Sonorense, or from Sonora:

> *Until 1853, southern Arizona was part of the Mexican state of Sonora, and to this day, those influences can be found north of the border. Dr. Jim Griffith draws an imaginary boundary that stretches about a hundred miles on either side of the border.*
>
> *Some families can trace their roots back to time before the changeover. Yearly fiestas celebrate historic events and religious holidays. Spanish is spoken in homes, schools, businesses and on the street. And as far as chimichangas are concerned, Sonora, Mexico, is one of if not the only place in Mexico where one might find a chimichanga on a restaurant menu.*

As Rick Bayless noted in the August 15, 1990 *New York Times* article "On the Trail of the Tortilla: All Trails Lead to Tucson," "Sonoran food is what Americans perceive of as Mexican food, and California Mexican food is based on Sonora."

We Can't Even Agree on How the Chimichanga Got to Be Called the Chimichanga

In Vera Cruz one tortilla is filled, rolled like a cigar and called a molote and in Nogales the rolled meat-filled snack staggers under the name chimichanga.

—The Food and Drink of Mexico, *George C. Booth*

Just how chimichangas came to be called chimichanga is another controversial topic. There is the El Charro story of a suppressed curse word and the Club 21 version where a comment by a customer ("how clever") eventually developed into "chimichanga."

For etymologists or at least some word mavens, the word is divided into two parts: *chimi*, the past participle of *chamusca*, meaning "seared," and *changa*, the third-person present of *chingar*, a vulgar expression for something not expected, a surprise.

Some others swear that the word is a mashup of two Spanish words: *chivo*, meaning "goat" (goat meat was commonly served in northern Mexico), and *changa*, which very loosely translates to a female monkey (not necessarily

FOOD WARS

Chimichangas are not the only food that stirs controversy when it comes to its origins. Several sandwiches, the Reuben and the French dip, each have disputed stories as to who created them and where they were created. Another classic food feud concerns the Philly cheesesteak, with two factions declaring that they were the first to make this iconic sandwich. The all-American treat, the banana split also has two cities with claims on its origin.

As far as the Reuben goes, the first story has roots in Omaha, Nebraska. According to Elizabeth Weil, it was her grandfather Bernard Schimmel who made the first Reuben. Schimmel owned the Blackstone Hotel in Omaha, Nebraska, where he and his friends held regular poker games. As often happens, the participants got hungry, and Schimmel went to the kitchen and put together a sandwich with corned beef, Swiss cheese, Russian dressing and sauerkraut for his friend, one Reuben Kulakovsky. The Kulakovsky family claimed that it was Reuben himself who put the sandwich together from the ingredients that were placed in front of him.

The second story belongs to a restaurant in New York City. Arnold Reuben opened his first restaurant, appropriately named Reuben's, in 1908 or so. But it wasn't until a move to a different space in 1935 that the beginning of the eponymous sandwich was created. One night in 1914, Annette Sealos, an actress, arrived at the restaurant with a ravenous appetite and pleaded with Arnold to make her a big, satisfying sandwich. The result was the Reuben, although notes say that the sandwich had turkey and ham and not corned beef.

Arnold's son, Arnold Jr., told his version of the story. He worked at his father's place from the early 1930s and always ate his meals there. The chef, Alfred Scheuing, decided to serve Junior something beside his usual hamburger, and making the most of ingredients he had on hand (fresh corned beef, Swiss cheese, thick rye bread and sauerkraut), he served Arnold Jr. his creation.

No mention is made of the Russian dressing. Junior claimed this was in the early 1930s.

The battle raged into the pages of the *New York Times* when Weil wrote a short piece telling her grandfather's story. Food writer Andrew Smith was on the side of the Big Apple, but eventually Weil found menus from the Blackstone dating from 1934 and 1937 with a Reuben on them.

Like the Reuben, the French dip has multiple people claiming to have made the first sandwich. The only point on which they agree is that it happened in Los Angeles.

Cole's story is customer inspired. In 1918, in order to help a customer who had difficulty eating the hard bread in Cole's roast beef sandwich, chef Jack Garlinghouse dipped the sandwich in au jus.

Phillippe's, another popular Los Angeles restaurant, noted that the sandwich was an accident by owner Philippe Mathieu. Much like the chimi accident, Mathieu dropped a beef sandwich in a pan of pan au jus and voila! That the main players from Phillippe's have other versions only complicates the issue. One has a firefighter complaining about the stale bread on his sandwich, so Phillippe dipped the bread in au jus and unceremoniously plopped it in front of the guy with a "like it or lump it" attitude. Another tells of a customer who simply asked for extra jus.

And if that isn't confusing enough, some say that the original French dip was made with pork.

As far as the Philly cheesesteak goes, Pat Molinari had been selling grilled hot dogs for a decade to hungry patrons out of his little truck. Out of boredom, he grilled some beef one day, plopped in an Italian roll and enjoyed it so much that he put it on his menu. This was sometime in the mid-1930s. Just across the street is Geno's, which claims that while it might be true that the first steak sandwiches were served at his neighbor's restaurant, it was Geno's that was the first to add the cheese. We won't discuss the provolone versus Cheez Wiz debate.

On the sweeter side of food battles, a friendly rivalry exists between Wilmington, Ohio, and LaTrobe, Pennsylvania. In 1907 in Wilmington, at The Café soda fountain, owner Ernest Hazard was looking for a way to grow his business, so he challenged his workers to create a new ice cream treat. But it was Hazard who came up with the idea of splitting a banana, topping it with three kinds of ice cream and an assortment of toppings. Every year, Wilmington holds the Banana Split Festival. The word is that when asked what it was called, he replied "a banana split."

The LaTrobe story has an apprentice pharmacist, David Strickler, as the creator of what he dubbed the banana split sundae. This was in 1904. So it looks like LaTrobe wins, but it should be noted that it was Strickler who built the famous long, narrow dish just for his creation.

Please note, we don't take sides with any of these stories.

in a family-friendly sort of way). Some translate the whole word to mean "toasted monkey."

A bar in Nogales, Mexico, called Chimi Chango was the inspiration according to one theory, although no one alive today seems to remember the bar. Another bar-inspired take has a barfly party boy named Jimmy holding huge parties (*pachangas*) at which he served baked burros, and people called them Jimmy's pacahngas, which morphed into "chimis changas."

Because the word itself can mean "thingamajig," one can almost imagine some worker pulling a deep-fried homemade burro from a lunch pail and when asked, "What the heck do you call that thing?" answers with a shrug, "I don't know, it's just a little chimichanga my wife cooked up this morning from the leftover burros from dinner last night."

CHIVICHANGA OR CHIMICHANGA?

Some people believe that the "chivichanga" is a precursor to a chimichanga or some type of variation.

In parts of Sonora, Mexico, people have been eating chivichangas for decades. The Yaqui Indians were said to have eaten them in Mexico before they made a forced move north to Arizona, bringing the dish with them.

Chivichangas can also be found in the bus station in Imuris, Mexico.

Rick Bayless, the Chicago chef and restauranteur, remembers eating chivichangas that were filled with goat meat in Baja, Mexico. Diana Kennedy, the British woman whom many consider the queen on "authentic" Mexican fare, has recipes for chivichangas in some of her cookbooks.

Technically, chimichangas and chivichangas have many of the same qualities: a protein, a flour tortilla and frying. But whereas a chimi is rolled and then deep-fried, the chivi is filled, folded into a square or triangle, pan-fried in some oil and then sometimes topped with mayonnaise and shredded cabbage.

IT'S NOT OFFICIAL—CHECK "YES!" FOR THE CHIMI

In his book *Chasing Arizona: One Man's Yearlong Obsession with the Grand Canyon State*, author Ken Lamberton explored the twelve official symbols of the state of Arizona. From the official gemstone (turquoise) to the official neckwear (the bolo tie) to the official firearm (the Colt single-action army revolver), Lamberton traveled the length and breadth of the state, talking with people, doing deep research and eating chimichangas, because although Arizona doesn't have an official food, he felt that the chimi was as symbolic of the Grand Canyon State as the official reptile (the ridge-nosed rattlesnake). As he has noted in a recent interview, "Chimis are what makes us who we are. They were invented here. We are the chimichanga."

WHEN A CHIMI ISN'T A CHIMI...OR IS IT?

While chimis can be found in the majority of Mexican restaurants in Arizona, not every restaurant calls their versions "chimichangas." Whether that clears up or confuses the issue is up for debate. Little Sombrero in Casa Grande doesn't list chimis on its menus, but you can get any of its burros fried for a small charge. At Maya's Restaurant & Sports Cantina in Parker in northern Arizona, they're called "chimichanga burritos"; the same term is used at Fiesta restaurants in Williams and Prescott Valley. In Yuma, Blaisdell's Steakhouse serves its burros chimichanga-style with a choice of either red or green sauce. Arturo's in Prescott calls them "fried burritos." In tiny Dewey, you'll find "Chimi Chongos" at Puerto Vallerta Restaurant.

The fact that Arizona doesn't have a state food isn't for lack of trying. In 2011, as part of an advertising campaign, Woody Johnson of Macayo's proposed the idea and with the help of the Flores family of El Charro began a campaign complete with an online petition to get the state legislature to make the chimichanga the official state food. Other restaurants and state legislator Kate Brophy McGee of Phoenix joined forces. After all, they argued, chimis were created here and at both restaurants chimis were top sellers.

An official food wasn't such an unusual concept. Most states, in fact, have several state foods that include official state pies, official state cookies, official state fruits and official state vegetables. Texas has ten different foods ranging from grapefruit to chili con carne. Maryland has the blue crab. Florida has the key lime pie. And Connecticut claims the steamed hamburger.

The restaurants found plenty of support in newspapers and on the street, but there was pushback, as people felt other foods were more representative of the state's culinary culture. Other suggestions included frybread, already the official food of North Dakota; *raspados*, a Mexican fruit drink; the Sonoran

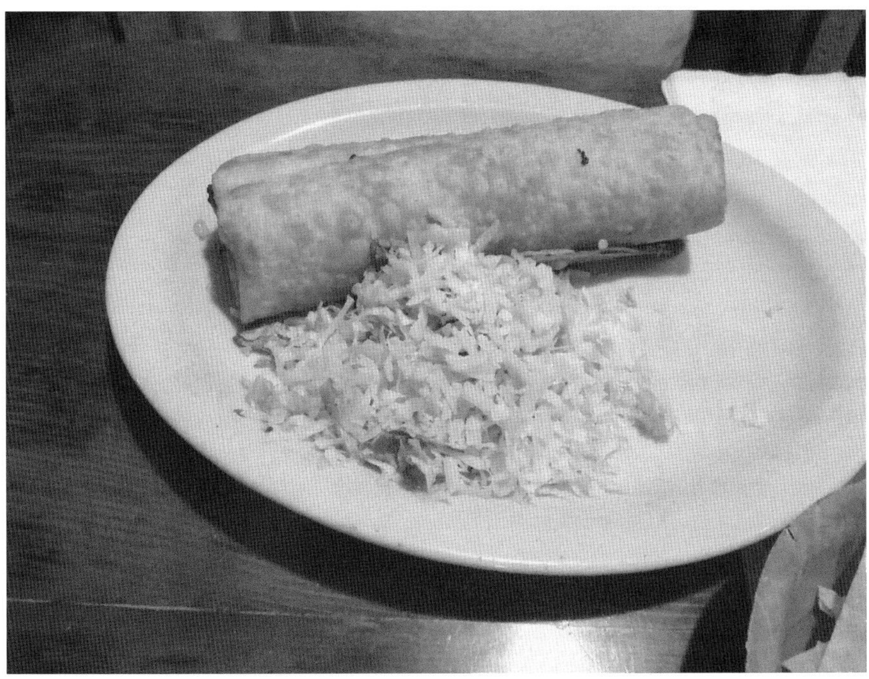

Micha's. *Author photo.*

hot dog, a popular street food found in Tucson and Phoenix; anything made from prickly pear (even though the Saguaro is our state cactus); T-bone steak from a state legislator; and ostrich, an argument that came from a chef who featured the bird on his menus. But nothing was quite as strongly supported as the chimichanga.

In 1997, when former baseball player and announcer Joe Garagiola was in Tucson for the PGA Open golf tournament named in his honor, he ordered a chimichanga at Pancho's but he called it a "chi-chi-chongo."

The idea eventually made its way to the state legislature, and here is where it all came to a screeching halt. In spite of the fact that Arizona was on the verge of celebrating its centennial in 2012, which folks argued was a great time to enact such an idea, the powers that be felt that the idea was frivolous considering all the more important issues like heavy state debt and a sluggish economy. There was also an election coming up.

The measure died a quick death and was never revived, although every now and then, you can hear the rumblings of others championing making chimichangas the official state food.

JUST WHAT THE HECK IS A CHIMICHANGA?

No dish better represents the Southwest than the chimichanga.
—Tom Miller, author of Revenge of the Saguaro

Chimichangas are composed of meat and vegetables rolled in a flour tortilla that is then deep-fried. All kinds of trimmings can be added on top. The only constant is the tortilla. Everything else is up to the chef or the diner.

Tortillas

The American capital of flour tortillas, though, is Arizona, where they are prepared in a manner virtually identical to that of the ones across the border in Sonora.
—Gustavo Arrellano, The New Yorker, *January 13, 2018*

During one of our trips to Toronto to visit our daughter and her family, we discovered that our bags were over the weight limit. The airline employee asked if we were carrying tortillas in our bags. We were—several dozen, actually—since good, true flour tortillas in Toronto are scarce. She laughed and said that it happens every day at the Tucson International Airport and let the overage pass.

Flour Tortillas

Although many will argue about the origins, flour tortillas are Sonorense, of and from Sonora. They aren't common in other parts of Mexico, where dining is exclusively on corn tortillas, and in different parts of the Southwest, flour tortillas are made in different ways. Although corn tortillas are used in Arizona for enchiladas and such, chimis require flour tortillas. Locals buy them warm and soft from neighborhood markets, tortillerias and family-run Mexican bakeries. Some restaurants make their own.

Wheat was first brought to the Southwest by Spanish missionaries in the late 1600s. They also brought cattle, which introduced beef to the diet of the natives living in the area. Both items became important staples in the native diets and are the basis for many Mexican dishes we still eat today.

Flour tortillas are abundant in Arizona and come in numerous sizes, from the smaller-than-your-hand size to the giant, thin tortillas that make the best chimis. Some eighteen inches in diameter, these tortillas are soft, chewy and delicious.

A simple combination of grain, water, some kind of fat and a touch of salt results in a soft, sticky dough. In the hands of an experienced tortilla maker, the dough is rolled into balls, the size of which depends on the size of the future tortilla. Then the hard part occurs. The transformation into a tortilla requires stretching, pulling and just the right amount of pressure—it's more art than anything. They are then plopped onto a large, ultrahot (six hundred degrees) cast-iron griddle called a comal. The breakdown of the gluten results in a tender, chewy tortilla. Sadly, the time-taking process is almost a lost art, as tortilla machines and flattops have taken over at many tortilla shops.

But even the machine-made tortillas are heavenly and have been compared to crepes, tissue paper and communion wafers. These tortillas are sometimes called *sobaqueros*, from the base word *sobaco*, or armpit. Depending on who you talk to the term is either high praise for the makers who artfully stretch the tortillas all the way from the tip of their fingers to the top of their arms; or a derogatory reference to unclean bodies. Another definition may come from the Spanish word for purse, which the tortillas resemble when wrapped around fillings. It's a class thing, but either way, Arizonans love their flour tortillas and will defend then to the last tooth.

It should be noted that the giant tortillas cannot be found in all parts of the state. Restaurants in the far reaches of the state use the next best thing: twelve-inch flour tortillas. The chimis may not be as big, but the flavor is not lost. For those with gluten issues, gluten-free tortillas are available at many restaurants. Vegans can find lard-free tortillas as well, although those are rarer.

One theory on the origin of the flour tortilla poses that they were brought to the West by crypto-Jews and Muslims who fled Spain due to centuries of persecution and settled in the western part of the United States and Mexico in the 1700s.

ST. MARY'S MEXICAN FOOD

St. Mary's Mexican Food makes 130 dozen tortillas every day. Known for its large *sobaqueros*, St. Mary's tortillas have been voted the "Best Tortillas" numerous years in a row (in the years it didn't win top honors, it usually came in second).

John Luis Salazar and his wife, Maria, opened their tiny shop just west of downtown in 1971. At first, they sold only tortillas and tamales to the neighboring homes but eventually added tacos, enchiladas, tostadas, flautas and other Mexican fare. Today, people can buy carne seca, red or green chili, birria, beans and more by the quart to make burros at home with the house-made tortillas.

The family, including grandson Luis Salazar, makes the tortillas in much the same way as it was done in the beginning, although the dough is no longer mixed by hand. Early every morning, the staff mixes the masa and places the dough in a specially designed press that creates several dozen balls of dough of uniform size. St. Mary's boasts that it is the only shop in town that stretches the tortillas by hand.

The dough rests for about fifteen minutes, and then the magic starts. Working as a team (some of the women have been there for more than thirty years), the tortillas are shaped. One woman pats the balls of dough into discs. Then two other women flip the dough between their hands, back and forth until the tortillas are stretched to about eighteen inches in diameter. They then place the tortillas on a specially made carbon steel griddle set at 450 degrees.

You can see the steam escaping as the water evaporates, creating golden brown patches. They quickly turn the tortillas for a few more seconds on the griddle. Meanwhile, they are stretching more tortillas, and as one tortilla is pulled off, another takes its place. The whole process takes less than a minute.

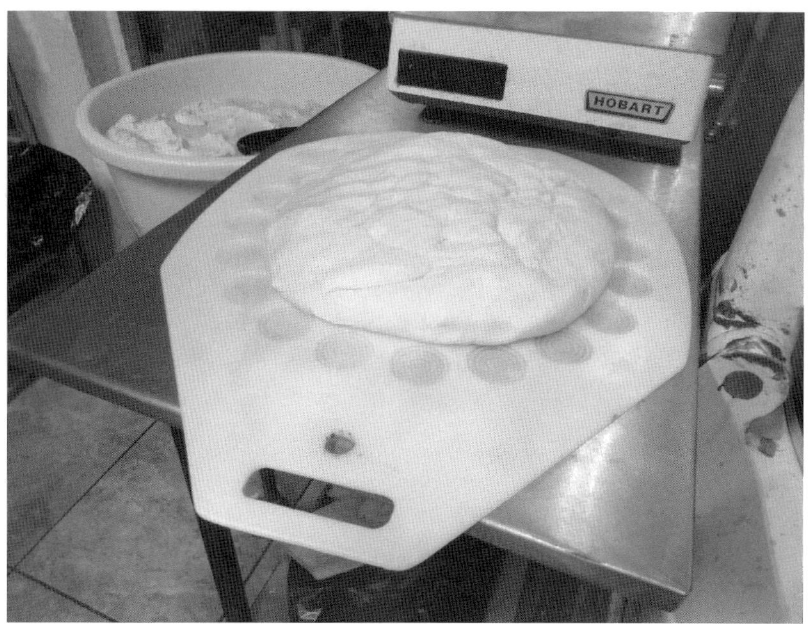

Making tortillas at St Mary's Mexican Food in Tucson. *Author photo.*

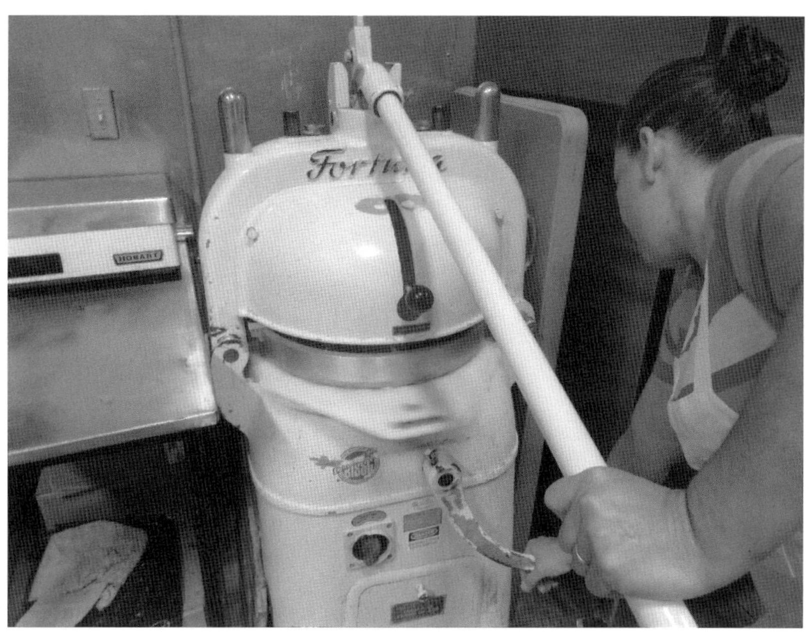

The dough is put in the press machine to create equal-sized balls of tortilla dough. *Author photo.*

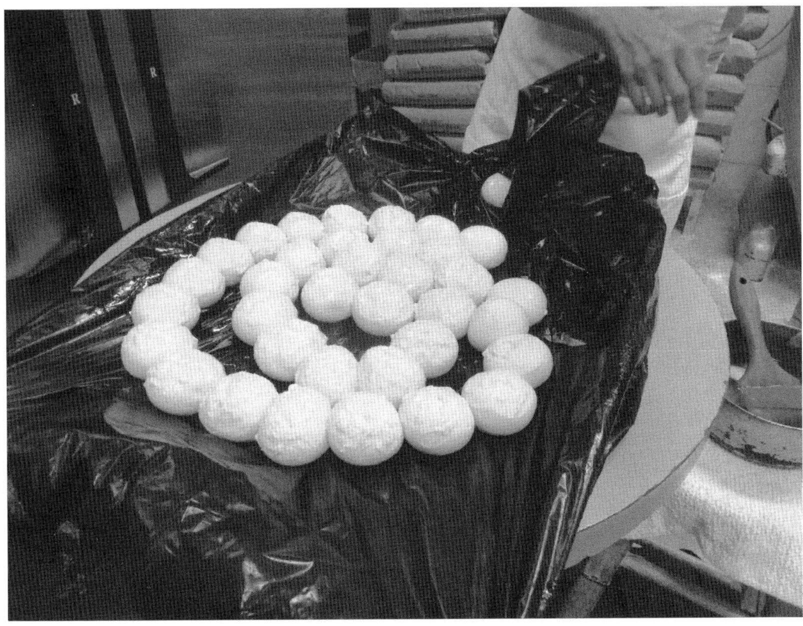

The dough balls. *Author photo.*

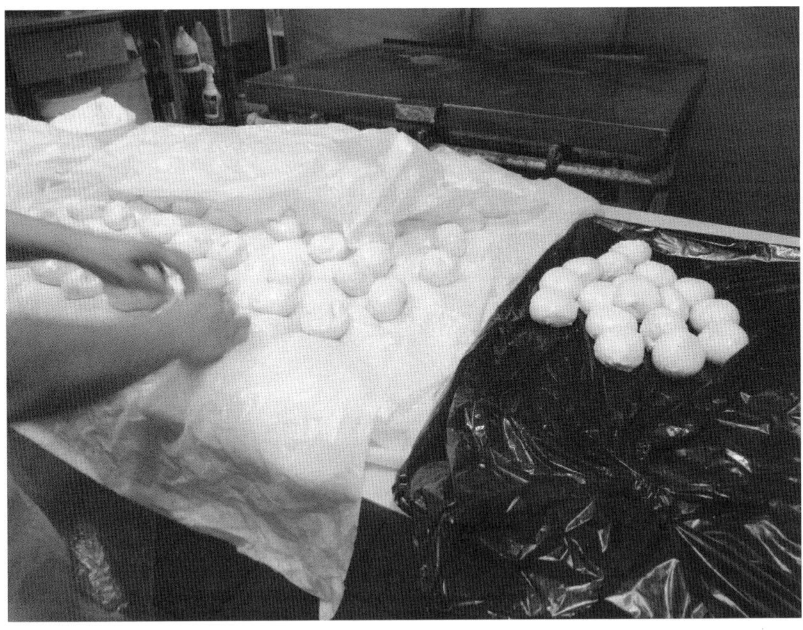

Patting the dough into a workable size. *Author photo.*

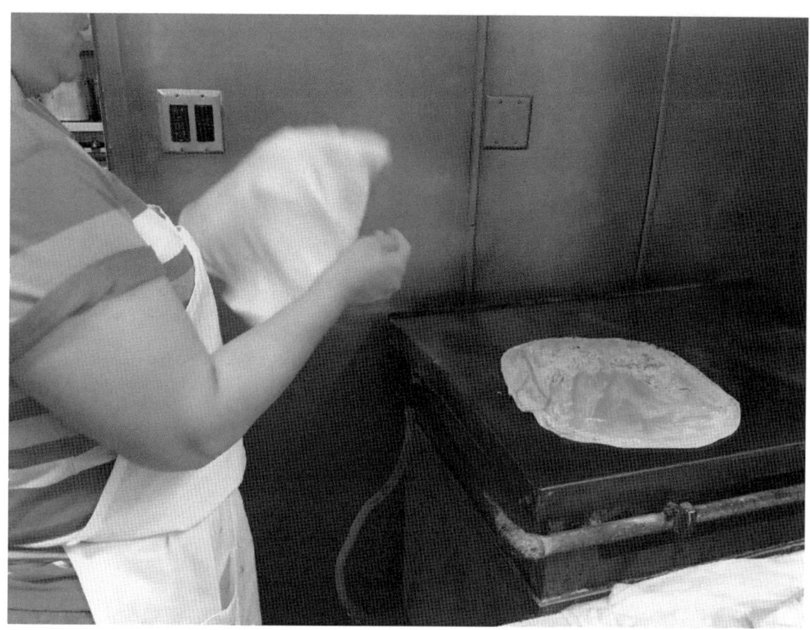

Stretching, spinning, stretching and spinning. *Author photo.*

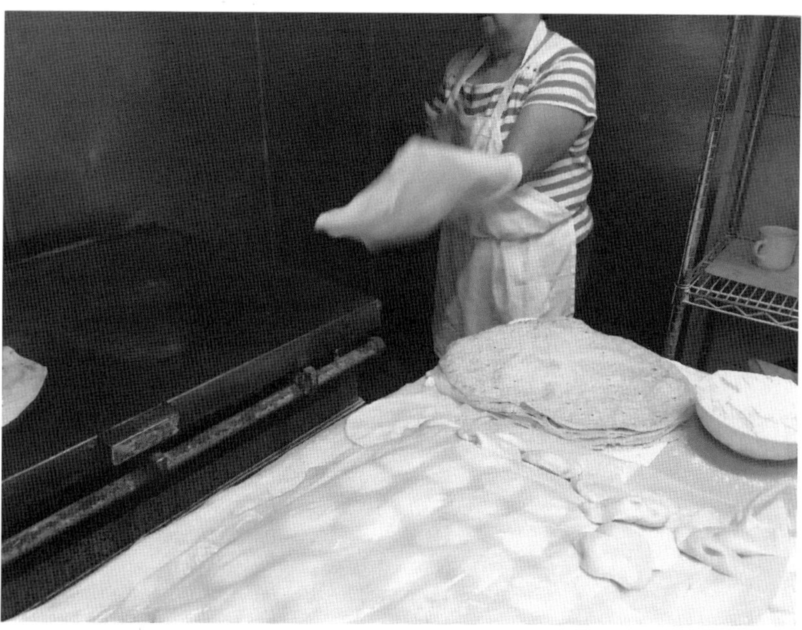

The tortillas are flipped back and forth as they are stretched paper thin. *Author photo.*

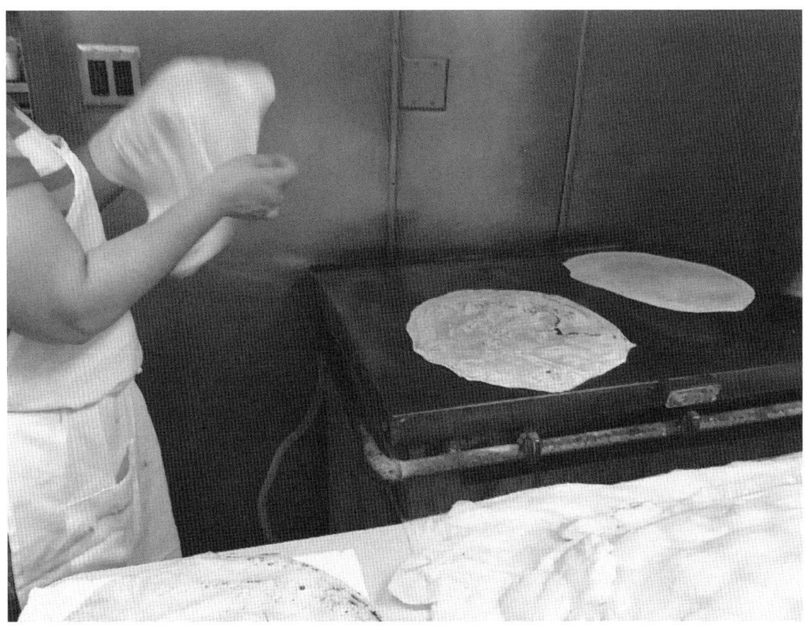

As one tortilla is cooked, another tortilla takes shape. *Author photo.*

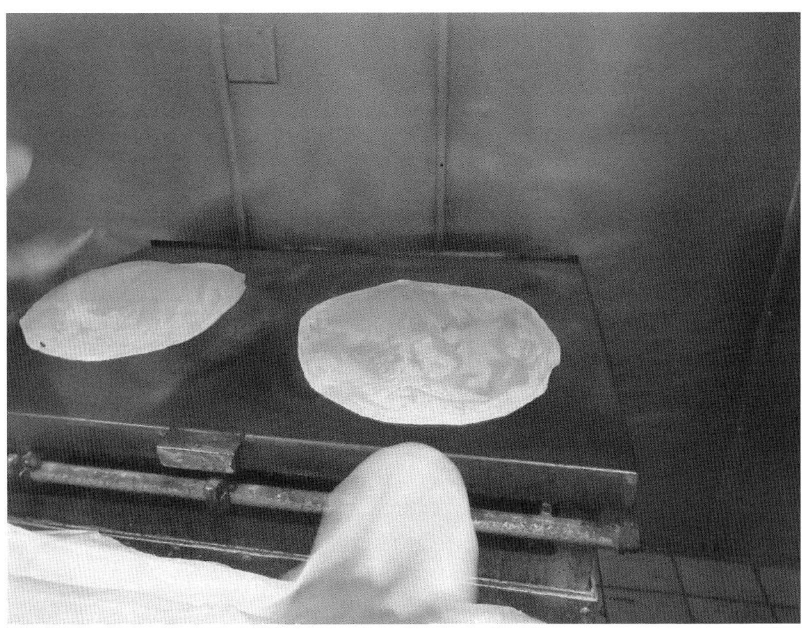

The tortilla spends only a few seconds on the griddle. *Author photo.*

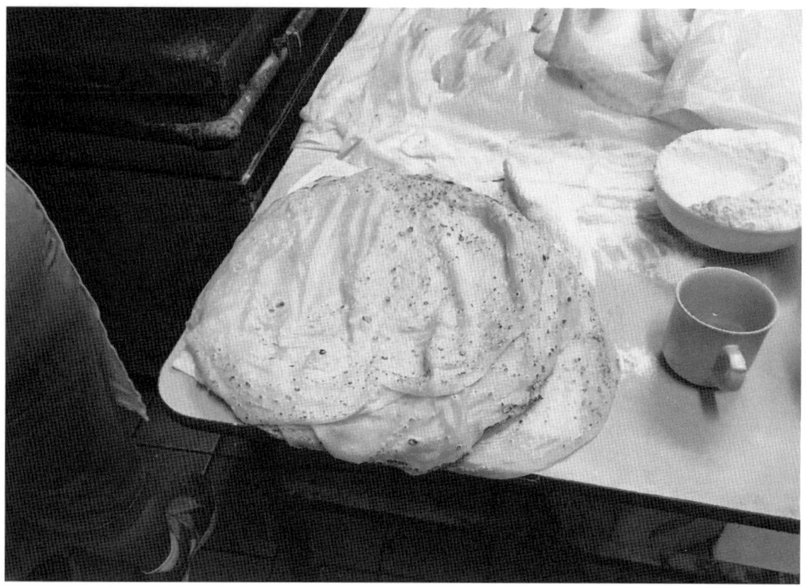

The final product: a stack of warm, soft tortillas. *Author photo.*

Watching the women create the tortillas is like watching a ballet. Each step flows into the next; muscle memory takes over, but there's nothing routine about the process. Love is in every tortilla.

The tortillas sell like hot cakes. People buy a dozen, two dozen or ten dozen. Former Tucsonans have been known to ship them all over the world. The photos included here show the work up close and personal.

While the red chile and carne seca chimis are big sellers, a specialty here is the chile relleno chimi.

NOT ALL TORTILLAS ARE ALIKE

An offbeat request resulted in a new way of looking at and eating tortillas when Javier and Esperanza Arevalo began making and selling tortillas after she lost her job following 9/11. The father-and-daughter pair along with wife and mother Matilde sold the tortillas at farmers' markets in Tucson and were doing quite well.

One day sometime in 2002, Gary Nabhan—currently the Kellogg Endowed Chair at the Southwestern Borderlands Food and Water

Security Department at the University of Arizona and one of the persons responsible for Tucson being named a UNESCO City of Gastronomy—asked them if they would make him some mesquite tortillas if he brought them mesquite flour.

Days later, the Arevalos were experimenting with the flour made from the pods of mesquite trees. They arrived at a workable product, one that was pliable for cooking and still had a great flavor. These tortillas are sweeter, a little smoky and darker in color. They are big sellers. Today, the tortillas are sold not just at farmers' markets but also health food stores and other stores in Tucson. They also ship anywhere in the United States.

Mayan legend tells the story of a peasant who created tortillas to honor the king. But these tortillas were made of corn, the most sacred food of the Mayas. Mayas believed that man came from corn and treated corn as sacred.

THE FINISHING TOUCHES

People have strong opinions as to what comes next once the chimi hits the plate. Salsa and cheese are de rigueur. But some insist that a chimi isn't a chimi unless sour cream and guacamole are involved in some way.

Others request some type of sauce—most often enchilada sauce, although many restaurants have their own special sauces. At Rosa's in Tucson, your chimi can be served Ortega style with the house's own cream-based sauce poured over the whole chimi.

Other restaurants also add their own touches, mostly in the form of some kind of cream sauce (crema) enhanced with everything including jalapeño peppers, cilantro, poblanos, tomatillos and more.

At Macayo's, the restaurant group with seven restaurants in the Phoenix area, there are several choices: the relleno, a tomato-based sauce; the fire-smoked tomatillo sauce; or the house enchilada sauce. Several restaurants serve Christmas chimis, which means they are topped with both red and green sauces.

And then there are the purists like Phoenix-based food writer Dominic Armato, who after eating twenty-four chimis in search of the best chimichangas in the Phoenix area made an impassioned plea to "please put the chimichanga on top of the sauce" because he feels the sauce makes the tortilla soggy and defeats the whole concept of a crispy chimichanga.

THE BIGGEST CHIMICHANGA IN THE WORLD

Micha's opened its doors in 1976, a latecomer of sorts when it comes to the restaurants found on South Fourth Avenue in South Tucson. South Tucson is the little city within the city of Tucson. One mile square, South Tucson has its own mayor, city council and police department. Many of the best and oldest Mexican restaurants can be found here, mainly on South Fourth, South Sixth and South Twelfth Avenues. For the most part, they've been around twenty, thirty, forty years and more. Most are still owned by the original families who opened them.

Micha's was opened by Gilberto and Artemisia Mariscal. The Mariscal family's restaurant was small, just a few booths and a counter, but as the decades rolled along, additions were made. With one of those additions comes the story of perhaps the largest chimichanga ever made.

In 1984, Gilbert Jr. and Richard Mariscal, sons of the original owners, wanted a special way to celebrate the latest expansion, and they decided to make the world's largest chimichanga. First, they had to get permission from the health department. Then they had a special stainless steel trough made and filled it with three hundred gallons of cooking oil.

Using a rectangular flour tortilla that measured sixteen feet in length, Gilbert and his crew filled and rolled the monstrosity into a tight cylinder on a mesh (also made of stainless steel) with handles. Ten hefty friends then carried the chimi outside to the parking lot, where a crowd of customers, the media and curious neighbors were waiting. Mariscal compared it to carrying a coffin or a stretcher with a heavy body on it.

The team carefully lowered the chimi into the hot oil. There's no record of how long it took to cook the chimi or how many people were on hand to eat it, but to this day, no one in the state of Arizona had ever attempted such a feat.

Today, Micha's, which is still owned by the Mariscal family, boasts some of Tucson's biggest chimis, although none come close to the Monster Chimi of 1984.

THE EXCEPTIONS TO THE RULE: BAKED CHIMICHANGAS

Deep-frying can only be successful if a great deal of fat is used.
—The New LaRousse Gastronomique
(Prosper Montigue, Crown Publishing)

By its very definition, a chimichanga is deep-fried, but a few restaurants have found a way around that while still producing some great chimis.

In Tucson, at El Saguarito, owner Albert Vasquez has been offering the "Healthy Mexican Food Alternative" (a term he has trademarked) for decades. Using canola oil ("Ola Canola" is another trademark) long before it became common, Vasquez makes not just healthful chimis but also tacos, enchiladas, fajitas, red chili, birria and just about every Mexican dish people love, but without the guilt.

El Saguarito first opened in 1989 in a reconverted El Taco stand on Tucson's northside. Several moves later, the restaurant is now located in central Tucson. The crowds followed.

The recipes come from Vasquez's first wife and her family, who owned La Fiesta in Douglas for decades. But his wife was a vegetarian, and when they opened El Saguarito, they wanted to stay away from animal fats. Using the family recipes and a little bit of ingenuity, they created dishes that she could eat.

All the tortillas used are made in-house without the lard that is found in most other flour tortillas. On certain weekends, customers can watch the tortillas being made in the restaurant.

The chimi fillings include some meat items like carne asada and red chili chicken, but everything is cooked in canola oil or, in some cases, no oil at all. There is a vegetarian option with zucchini, beans, corn, tomatoes, cheese and onions. The California chimis have either carne asada or grilled chicken, as well as potatoes, guacamole, cheese and the house pico de gallo. They are then "rolled" on the griddle with a minimum of oil. The texture may not be quite as crunchy as fried versions, but they are not as greasy either and they taste great.

Chimichanga was an answer to a question on the TV game show Cash Cab.

For many years at Chalo's Casa de Reynoso, owned by Chalo and Juanita Reynoso, the chimis were baked. "We used to do it in oil, but the oil was so expensive, so we buttered them and then

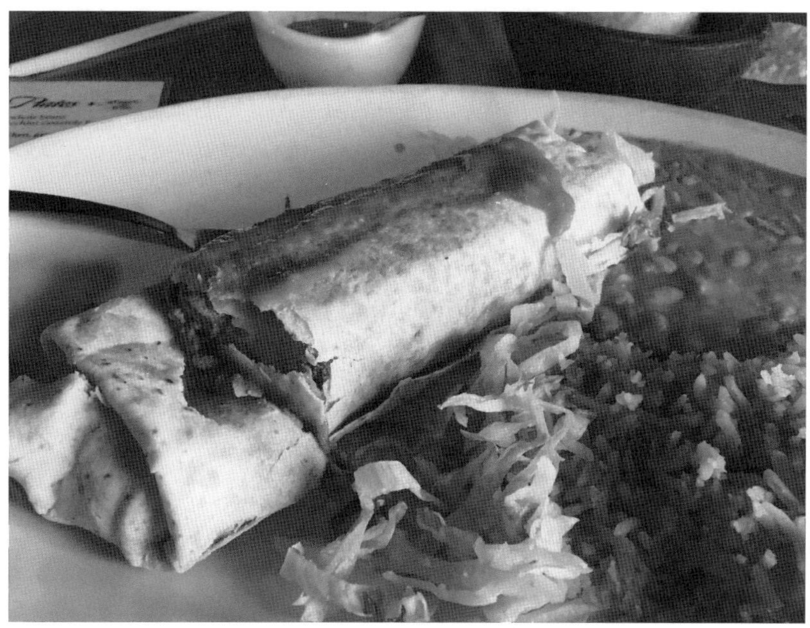

El Saguarito proves that a chimi can be tasty even if it isn't deep-fried. *Author photo.*

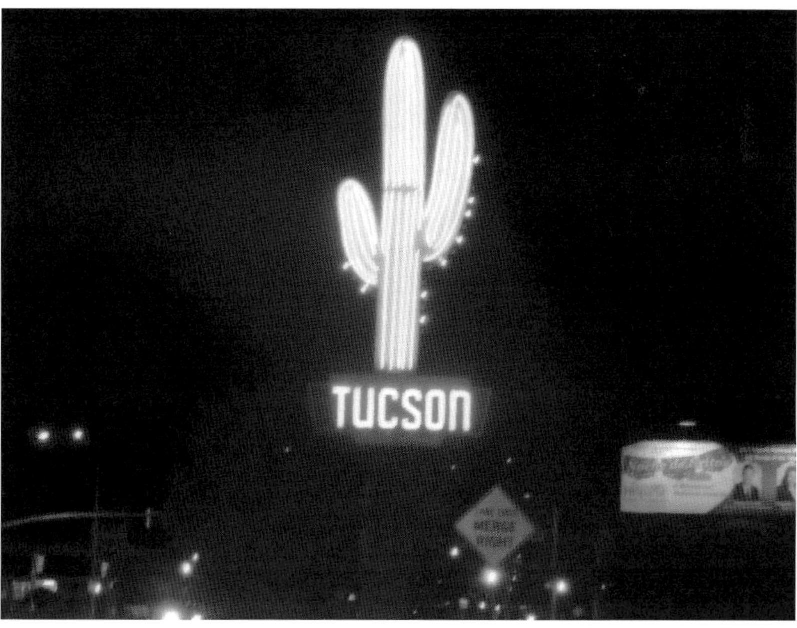

The glowing Saguaro cactus welcomes everyone to Tucson. *Author photo.*

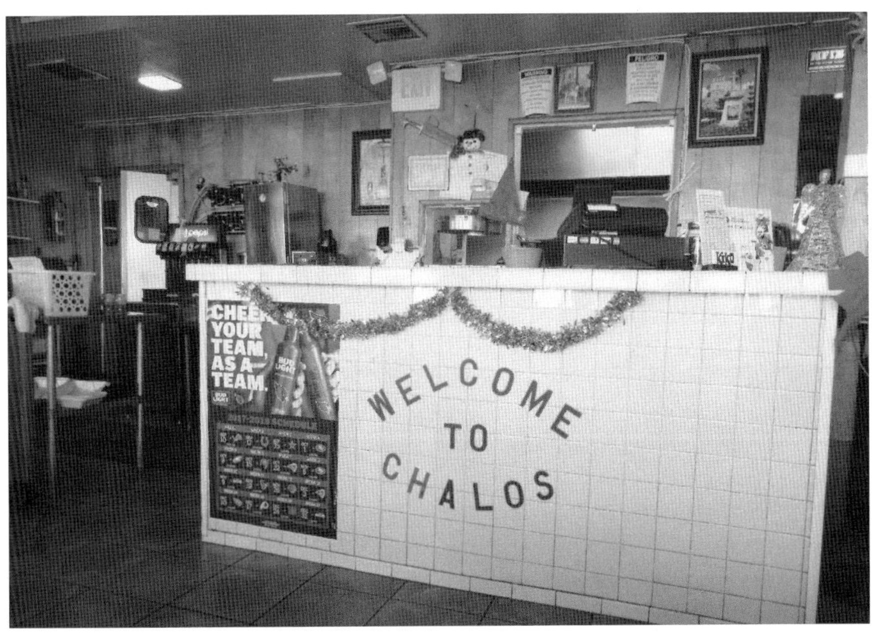

Chalo's in Globe welcomes you! *Author photo.*

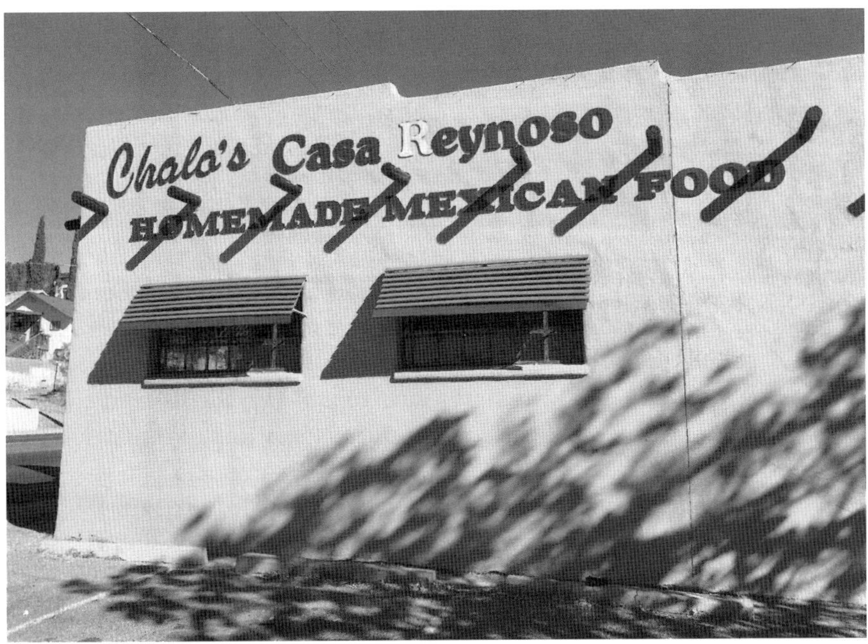

The exterior of Chalo's Casa Reynoso. *Author photo.*

baked them," said Juanita in a recent interview. But in the past few years, customers began asking for fried chimis, and so Chalo's went back to the old ways.

Their son, JR, sticks with the old ways and bakes his chimis at J&R El Rey in Globe. The "J" is for Junior and the "R" is his wife, Roberta. Roberta said that Junior feels that the oil changes the flavors of his green chili and other fillings and that oil overpowers the chimi, so he bakes them instead. Once the chimi is filled and wrapped, he slathers the item in butter and then bakes it on a flat pan in the oven. Baking takes a little longer, but Junior truly believes that this method allows for his flavors to shine.

MINI-CHIMIS

Chimichangas are almost always described as large or a synonym thereof. But truth be told, some of the best chimis found are small versions, or mini-chimis. Mini-chimis are usually dessert chimis, and some can be quite decadent. But savory versions, like with refried beans, carne seca and shredded chicken, are also common and are usually served as *antojitos* or *botanas* (appetizers).

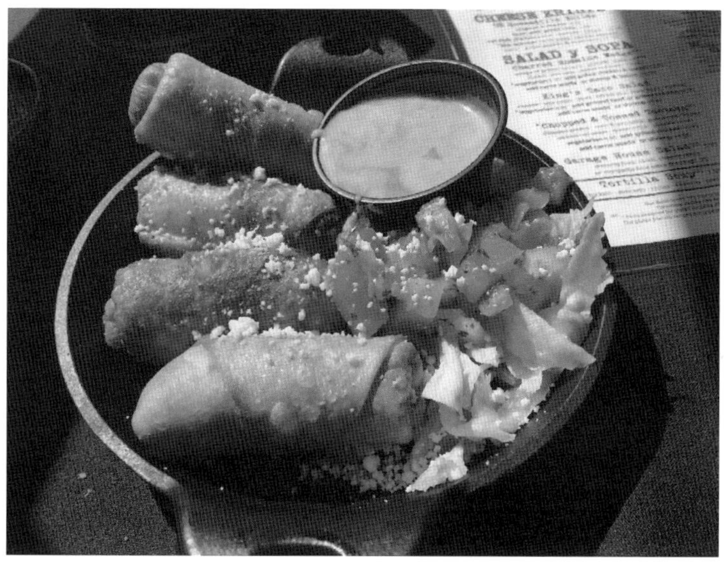

Sir Veza's mini-chimis. *Author photo.*

CHIMICHANGAS NEAR AND FAR

I'm surprised chimichangas were not Elvis' favorite deep-fried treat.
—David Fitzsimmons, Arizona Daily Star *editorial cartoonist*

TUCSON AND BEYOND

Tucson is a city with a rich culinary history. As far back as four thousand years ago, the area supported agricultural sites where Native Americans grew corn, beans and other crops.

In 1775, Hugo O'Conor claimed the land along the Santa Cruz River in the name of Spain. As Tucson grew from a tiny walled pueblo to a rough-and-tumble western town to a modern city with a savvy and clever culinary scene, food has played an important role.

Historical events brought culinary influences from Spain, Mexico, Native America, the Deep South and even the Far East, when Chinese railroad workers tired of the hard labor and miserable wages moved to Tucson to open restaurants and neighborhood markets. These influences are still a daily part of Tucson.

The University of Arizona and Davis Monthan Air Force Base are important players in the city's vibe. Both modern and historic, Tucson has plenty to offer for families, seniors, millennials, newcomers and lifelong residents.

In 2015, Tucson was named America's first UNESCO City of Gastronomy as part of the agency's Creative City Network. Taking into account ancient roots, multicultural influences, a commitment to food security and blossoming dining scene, Tucson was an ideal choice.

Did chimichangas have anything to do with Tucson receiving this prestigious honor? Chimi lovers in Tucson would no doubt say yes.

Micha's

The chimis they serve at Micha's may not be as big as the one they made in their attempt at the world record, but some folks claim they are the biggest in Tucson. That's no exaggeration: chimis here fill the plate to overflowing. There's a legend that a customer way back when ordered two chimis but left in disgrace when he realized that perhaps he'd overestimated his extreme eating talents.

Micha's was opened in 1976 by Gilbert and Artemisia (Micha) Mariscal in a tiny building on South Fourth Avenue in South Tucson. The place, formerly called the Rocket Restaurant, consisted of a few tables and a counter (a total of thirty-six seats) where folks could watch their food being prepared. They called it Micha's G&M (Gilbert & Micha). Only old-timers still use the full name. Artemisia did all the cooking, adding American breakfasts as an aside.

In the early years, it was only open for breakfast and a late lunch (it closed around 4:00 p.m. it they ran out of food and had to close early). Rooms were added as needed (it was as a celebration of one of the expansions that inspired the quest for the record chimi). Today, there are five rooms, each with its own feel. A shrine honoring Micha and Gilbert dominates the tiny lobby.

On the night of April 14, 2018, a huge fire ripped through Micha's restaurant, destroying the roof and causing irreparable damage to the interior. While much of the restaurant was destroyed by flames, smoke and water, the small shrine honoring founders Gilbert and Artemisia that stood in the lobby was left untouched. The photos of son Richard were also kept intact. The family vowed to rebuild. In June 2018, the Micha's team opened a food truck in a parking lot across the street from the original building. Although currently they only sell burros and tacos in the temporary eatery, plans to add chimichangas are in the works, with hopes to reopen the full restaurant before the end of 2018.

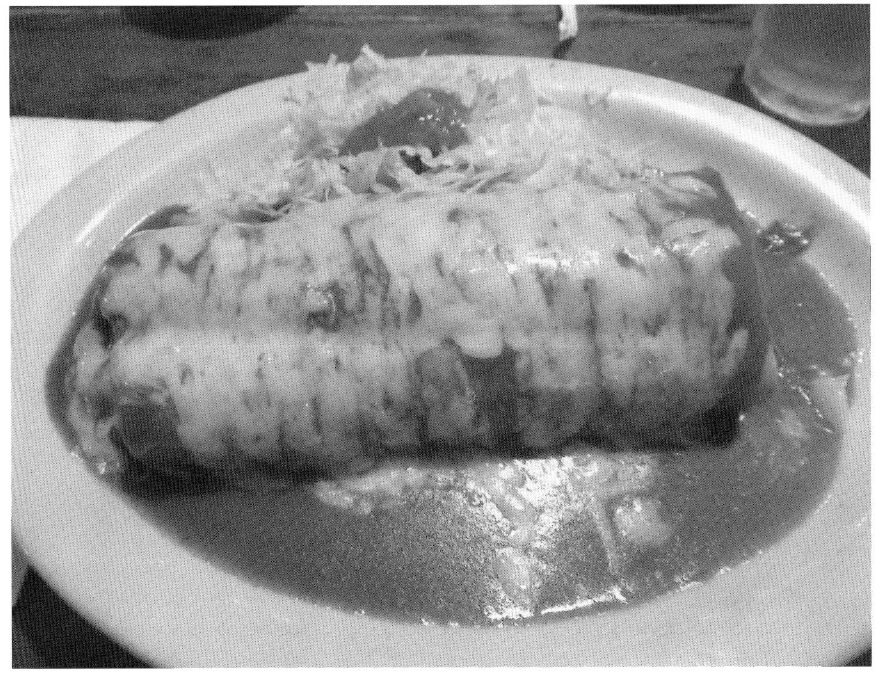

A chimi from Micha's is a big chimi. *Author photo.*

Gilbert and Micha weren't young kids when they decided to open their own restaurant. Gilbert had been a house painter, but after a serious fall in which he hurt his back, he had to "retire." Micha had run a successful maternity store. But with eight children and numerous other relatives, they made a go of it.

Son Richard took over running the restaurant as his parents aged. During his tenure, Richard expanded the restaurant and mentored numerous employees who went on to open their own successful restaurants: Rigoberto Lopez of two Rigo's restaurants; Daniel Contreras of two nationally recognized places called Guero Canelo; and Benjamin Galaz, who owns a casual BK Hot Dogs and El Berraco, a Latin seafood restaurant. The Mariscals were also known for their support of local baseball and softball teams, boxing events and numerous causes in South Tucson.

David Fitzsimmons, the political cartoonist from the Arizona Daily Star*, called the machaca chimis at this South Tucson restaurant "fat as a Yule log. Machaca eggroll on steroids."*

Over the decades, Micha's chimis have won numerous "Best of Tucson" titles. A third generation keeps the Mariscal traditions alive. On any given day, diners include government workers, nanas and tatas, families and longtime regulars.

Folks argue over which chimi is the best. The red chili has its fans, but the shredded beef with just a whisper of lime marinade also holds its own. The only way to determine the winner is to try them for yourself, but bring a friend or two because like we said, the chimis at Micha's are *big*!

MI NIDITO

Mi Nidito means "my little nest," and when it first opened in 1952, it was indeed small. With just a dozen tables and the restrooms outside, this restaurant was the definition of cozy. The tables were filled from day one. The place has expanded twice over the years, and the bathrooms have been indoors for quite some time.

Alicia and Ernesto Lopez had moved to Tucson from Sonora with plans to open either a tortilla factory or a restaurant. There was much discussion. Alicia was all for opening a place where she could cook up her recipes. Ernest thought that a tortilla factory would be a better idea.

Folks in Tucson are glad things worked out the way they did, and the proof shows up on any given evening (or lunch for that matter), when people happily wait more than an hour for a table.

Ernesto's son, Ernesto, and his wife, Yolanda, took over the restaurant in the 1960s. Grandsons Jimmy and Ernesto III run the place now and still serve Alicia's recipes, most famously her birria, to the throngs that gather. Recently, they obtained a special liquor license that allows people waiting on the patio to order one of the famous margaritas.

As people wait, they can look at the many photos of famous guests. The roster includes David Crosby, Julio Iglesias, Jim Belushi and President Bill Clinton. As expected, it was quite the big deal when the president arrived. He'd been in town for an event at Davis-Monthan and told the waitress that he was really hungry, so they put a special plate together. It didn't contain a chimi, but it did have just about one of everything else on the menu: a bean tostada, a chicken enchilada, a beef tamale, a chile relleno, a birria taco, beans, rice, guacamole and some slices of a cheese crisp. Today, the Presidential Plate is a featured item on the menu.

Another famous visitor was the Food Channel's Adam Richter. He filmed an episode of *Man vs. Food* in 2009. His review of the birria was, "MMMMMMM!"

EL MINUTO

El Minuto is a longtime favorite of Tucsonans. Opened in 1936 by John Shaar, the restaurant is located just south of downtown proper and across form the Tucson Convention Center.

Shaar was from Lebanon and had spent time in El Paso before moving to Tucson and opening El Minuto. The locals called him Juan. Today, Teresa Shaar, John's granddaughter, and great-granddaughter Zulema Salinas keep the tradition going. And while they've expanded the menu some since the early days (tacos, burros, beans, rice and menudo on weekends), the food here is much like it was back in the 1930s. No one is sure when chimis first appeared on the menu.

The story of El Minuto is one of perseverance and passion. In 1944, federal road construction forced the family to relocate the restaurant a few blocks east, next to the family home. That home was also torn down in the 1970s. In a fit of urban renewal, the City of Tucson tore down barrio homes and small businesses near El Minuto to build a shiny new community center. Mexican, Chinese and African American families were displaced without so much as a "sorry."

The business suffered not just because of the construction but because Main Street, the easiest way to get to El Minuto, was cut off by the construction; people assumed because they couldn't get to the place that the restaurant closed.

By this time, John's son George and his wife, Rosalva, were running the restaurant. Business was so bad that George had to take a second job. But they persevered mainly because, as Teresa put it, "We love the restaurant business."

And people love El Minuto. The location across from Tucson Convention Center means acts that play there often stop by after a concert. The photos on the wall show everyone from ZZ Top to Liberace. But on most nights, the place is filled with families, groups of friends, tourists and longtime Tucsonans, all seeking good-old fashioned Sonoran food.

George was killed in an auto accident while on the way home from another restaurant they had in Green Valley. Rosalva thought it best to sell

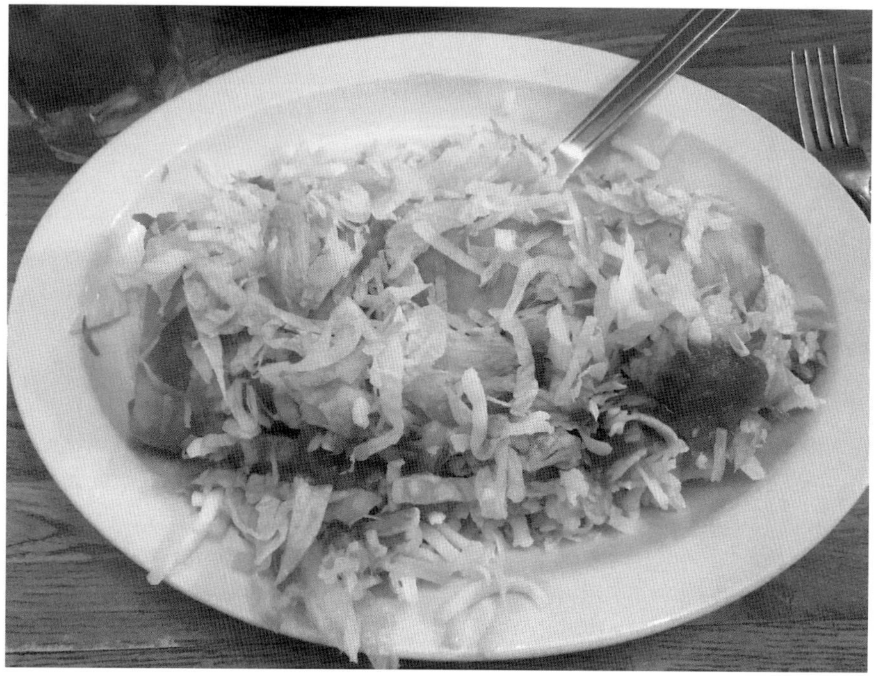

Red chili chimi from El Minuto. *Author photo.*

that site and concentrate on El Minuto with the help of her kids, George Jr., Teri and Michael.

George Jr. died in 2016, and Rosalva retired in 2017. Flavors here are the flavors of old-time Tucson Mexican restaurants, but no lard is used, as customers' tastes have turned away from unhealthful ingredients. Somehow, though, the beans taste the same, the enchiladas are still spicy and the chimis are as crispy as can be. The chimis are gigantic, with the most popular choices being the carne seca chimi and the red chili chimi.

CASA MOLINA

The Molina family has been serving fine Mexican fare since 1947, when Gilbert Molina, who owned a construction company, opened a tiny restaurant on what was then the edge of town. He built the restaurant so his sister, Maria, would have a way to support her family after a divorce. Not only did he make each of the adobe blocks for the building himself, but he

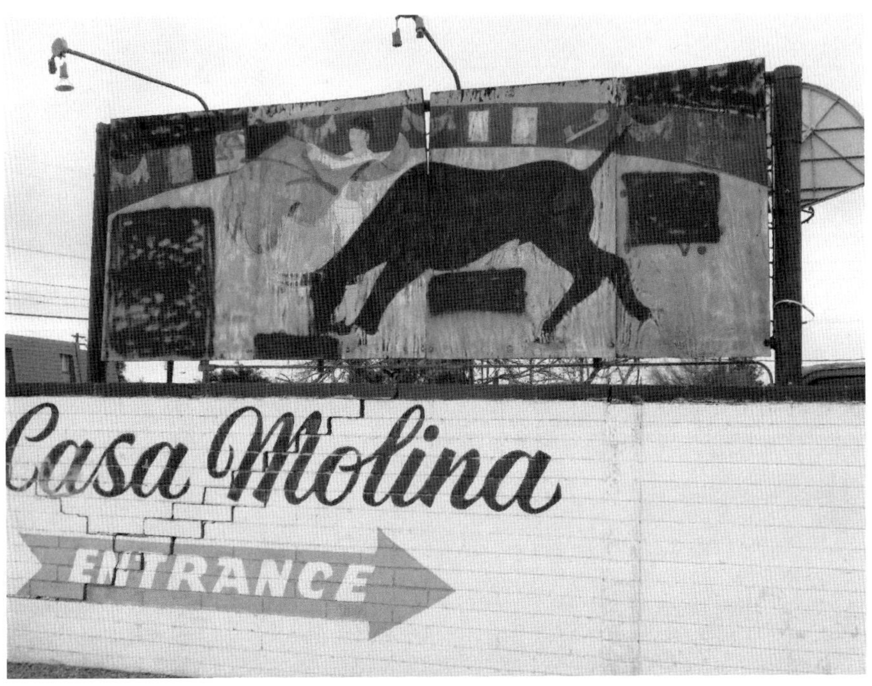

The sign of the bull means you're at Casa Molina. *Author photo.*

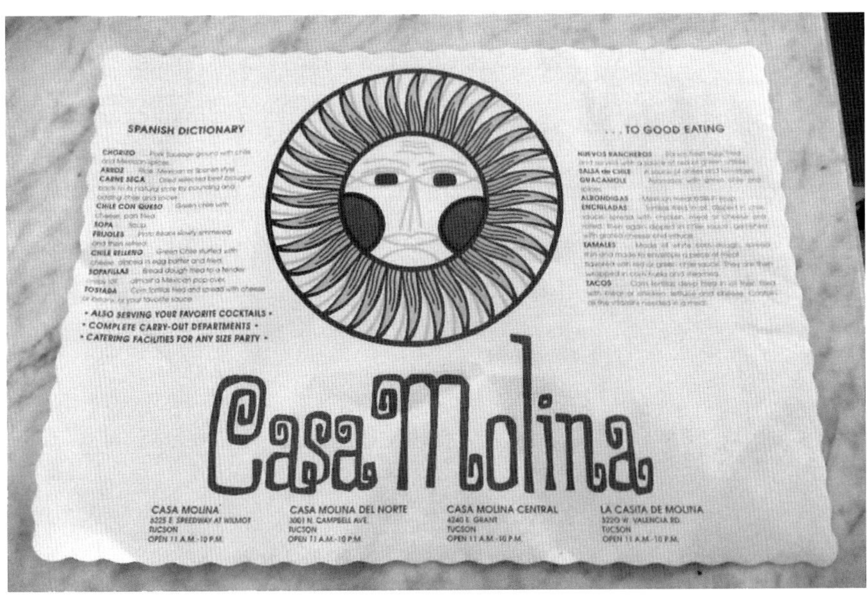

Casa Molina placemat. *Author photo.*

also made the chairs and tables. There was a total of sixteen seats. Today, the size has more than quadrupled.

As Tucson and the Molina family grew, other members opened their own Casa Molinas in various parts of town, most notably Midway Molina's, which was a favorite of Paul and Linda McCartney when they lived in Tucson. Sadly, Midway Molina closed in 2017, but the other restaurants are going strong.

The chimis here are a little different than most—long, narrow and ultra-crispy, inspired by Gilbert Sr.'s trips to Nogales, where he first saw chimis being served at La Frontera Bar. Today, a third and soon to be fourth generation of Molinas are running the five restaurants.

Club 21

Club 21 is a longtime local favorite and has been serving some version of chimichangas since it was opened in 1946 by George Jacob. The place started out as a tiny eatery on Miracle Mile, the strip of street that was home to dozens of tiny motor courts in early and mid-twentieth-century Tucson.

On the menu, burros are listed, with the choice of having them prepared chimichanga style. While all the usual options are offered, diners can also get a chorizo with egg chimi, which is often only found at breakfast at other places. On the Especiales de Casa part of the menu, there is an option called

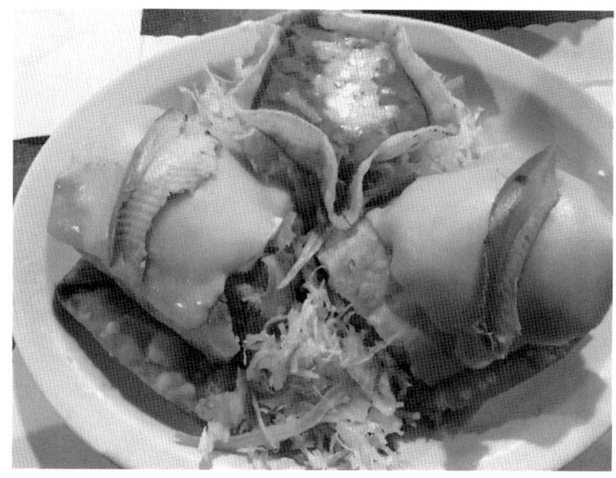

Chimichanga del Sol from Club 21. *Author photo.*

Chimichanga del Sol. Filled with either "prepared" chicken or barbacoa, the Del Sol is topped with a kicked-up cream cheese sauce and plenty of melted cheddar. The mix of flavors and textures make this especiale a treat.

Phoenix and the Valley of the Sun

As the capital of Arizona, Phoenix has grown to the fifth-largest city in America. Sparkling and sprawling, the city offers just about anything and everything people want and need. Shiny new buildings are framed by rugged mountain views. Major sports teams include a full slate of baseball spring training, as well as football, basketball and hockey teams. The resorts are world-class. An eclectic mix of museums, a thriving arts scene, a major university—Arizona State—and plenty of family activities are what Phoenix is all about.

Incorporated in 1881, Phoenix is a relative newcomer when it comes to cities in Arizona. Its roots spring from Fort McDowell. The fort needed hay and hay needed water, so John Swilling saw an opportunity to provide that water via a series of canals, much like the ones that the Hohokam tribes created around 500 BC. The Hohokams were one of the first native tribes to establish permanent farming in the area; until that time, most native groups had been nomads. Weirdly, the Hohokams disappeared in about 1450, and no one knows why or how.

Because of Swilling's great idea, more and more people were attracted to the area, and eventually the Yavapai County Board of Supervisors created the town (Maricopa County didn't exist at the time) on May 4, 1868. At a size of 320 acres, none of the 250 odd souls living there could have imagined the Phoenix of today. The name, some say, comes from the idea that the area was born again with the coming of the canals, just like the mythical bird.

Many communities have sprouted up around Phoenix, and while they are cities and towns with their own mayors and governments, they are included as part of "the Valley," a term used to define the entire area.

Each had its own distinctive characteristics. Scottsdale is posh with a high-end lifestyle. Tempe, home to Arizona State University, is a college town with all the trimmings. Mesa, once known for large farms, has transformed itself into a place to visit all on its own. And dining options range from James Beard Award–winning restaurants to tiny taquerias.

Phoenix will surprise first-time visitors, but residents know that their city is one of a kind.

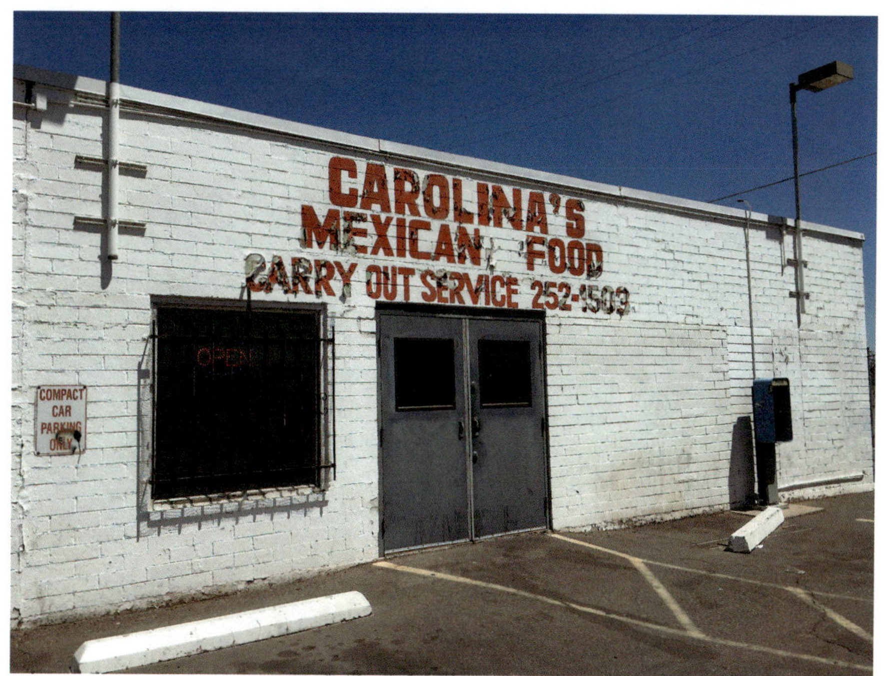

The legendary Carolina's. *Author photo.*

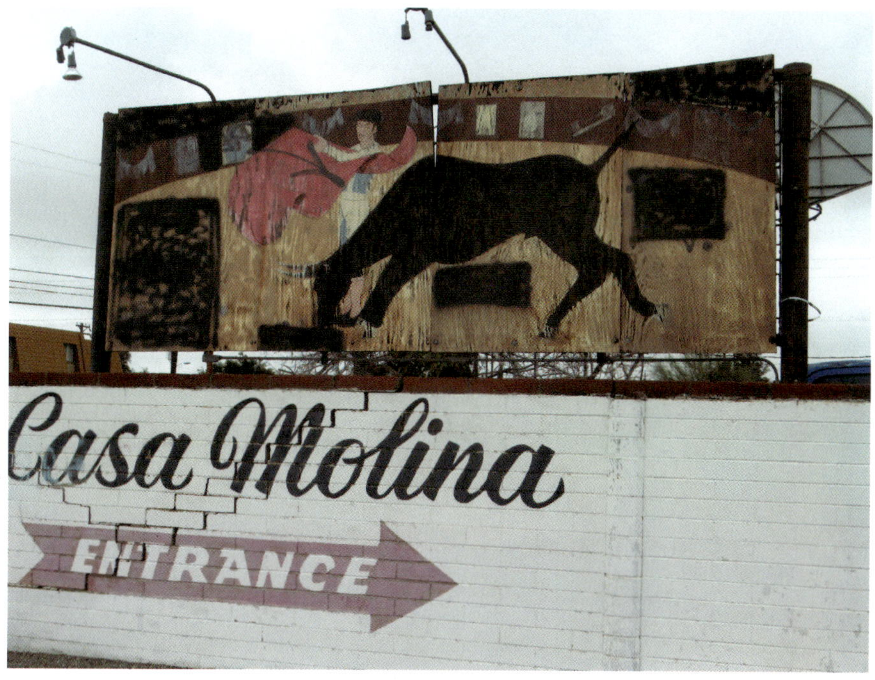

The sign of the bull means you're at Casa Molina. *Author photo.*

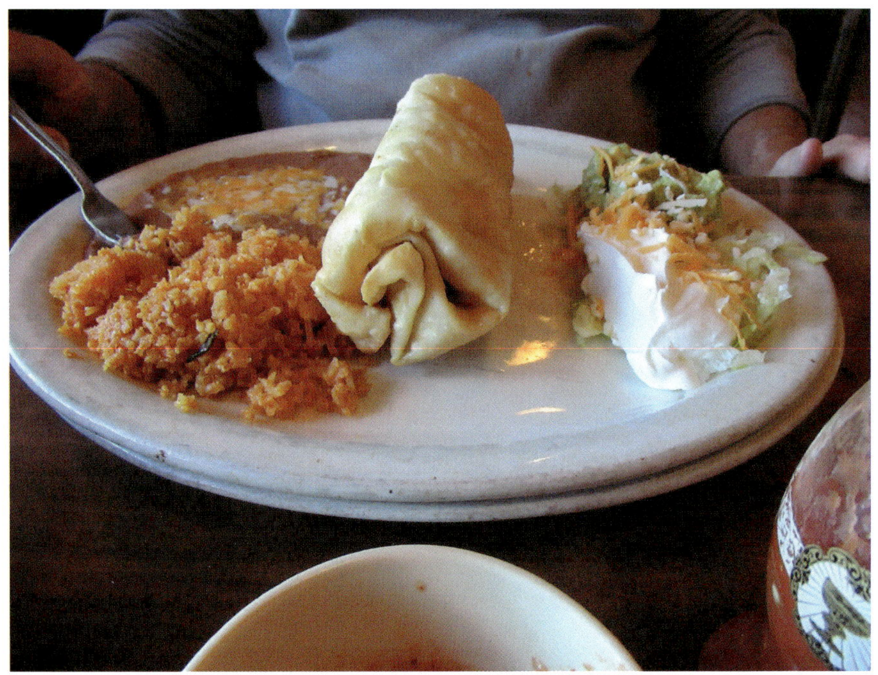

Another Reynoso chimi. *Author photo.*

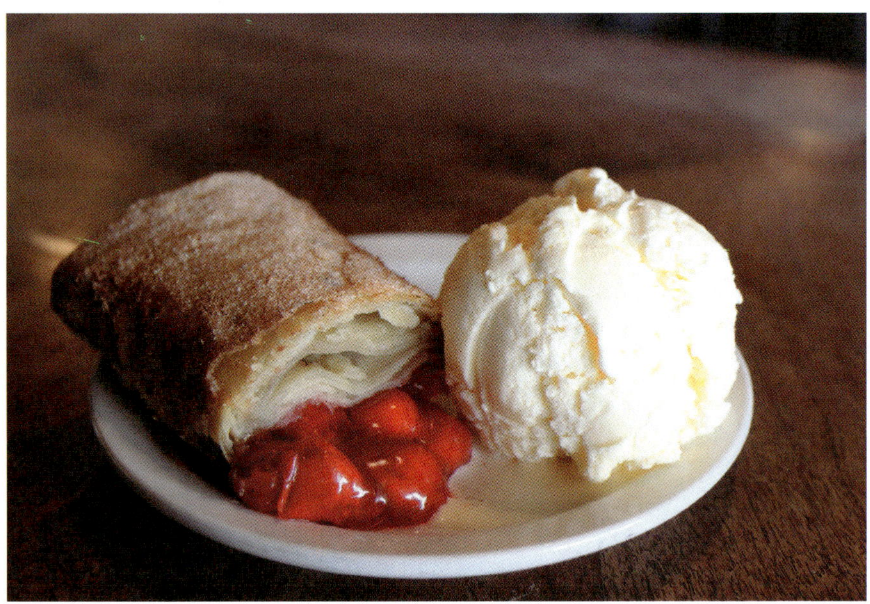

A cherry chimi unlike any other. *Courtesy Wisdom's Café.*

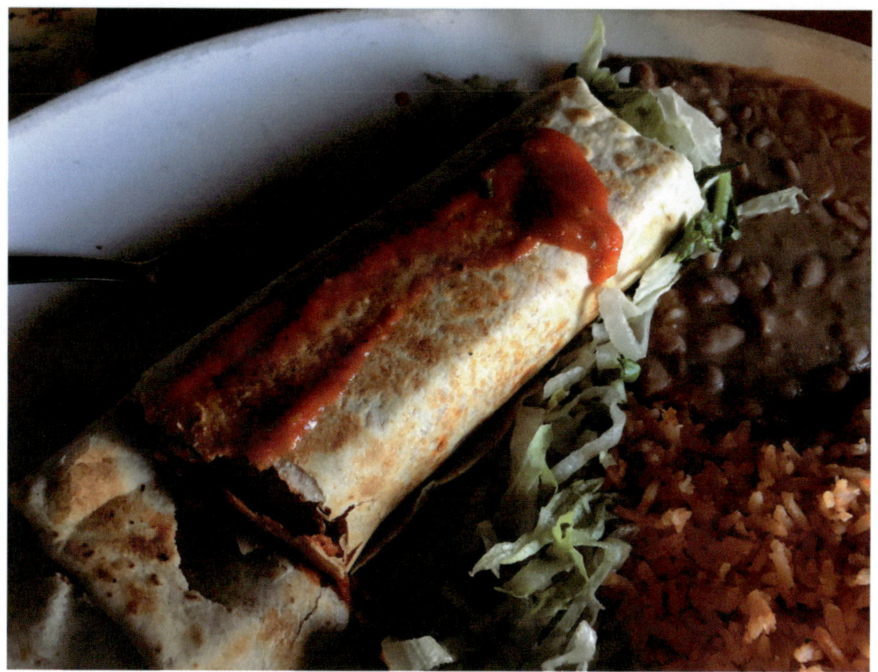

A grilled chimi from El Saguarito. *Author photo.*

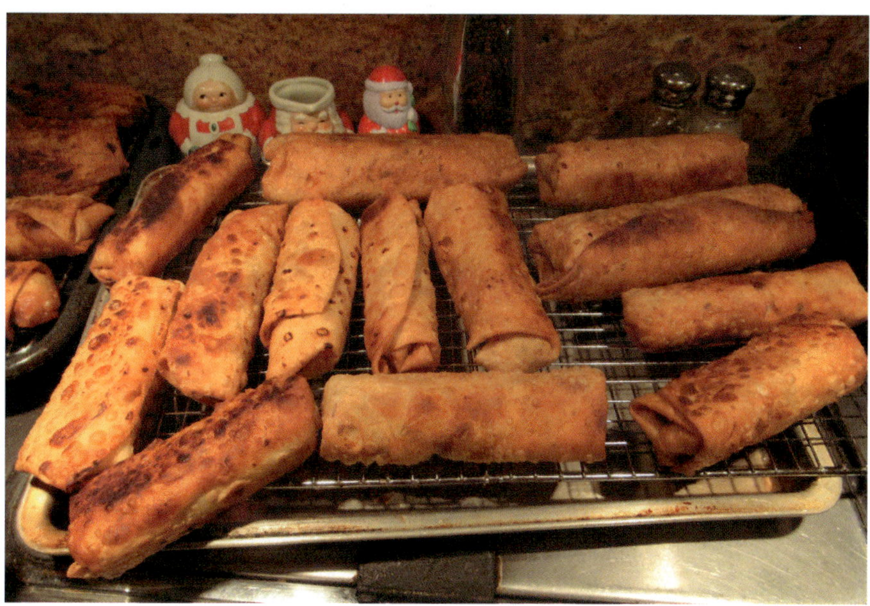

More delicious homemade chimis. *Author photo.*

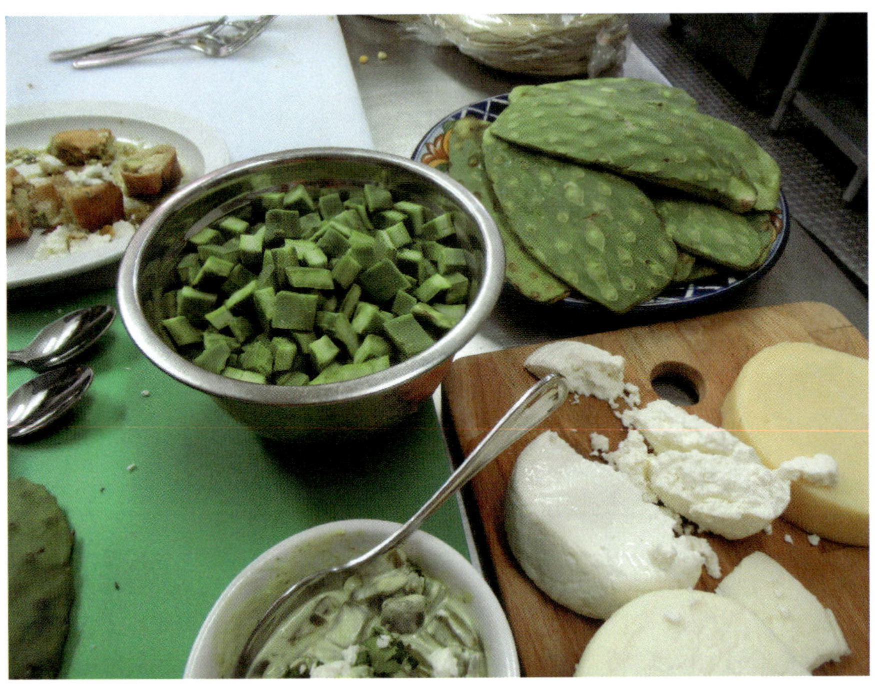

Nopales, or cactus pads, are cooked in numerous ways. *Courtesy El Charro.*

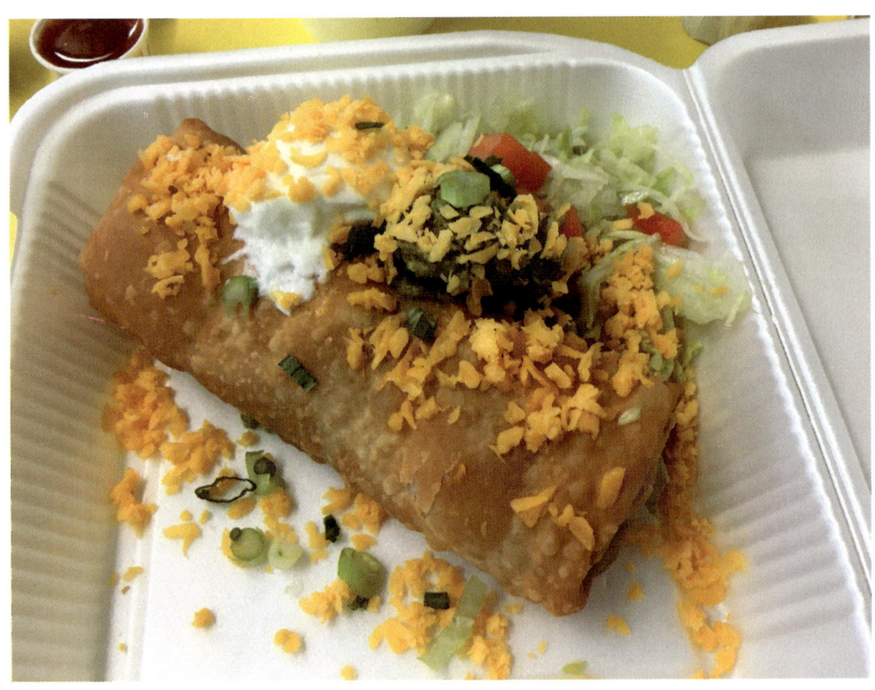

Carolina's superb chimis are all served in Styrofoam. *Author photo.*

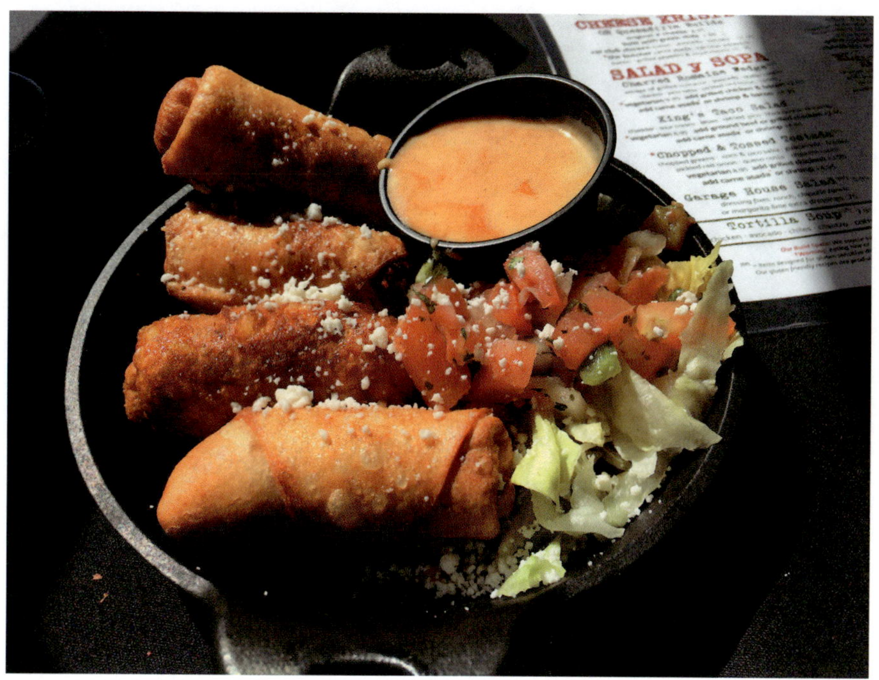

Sir Veza's mini chimis. *Author photo.*

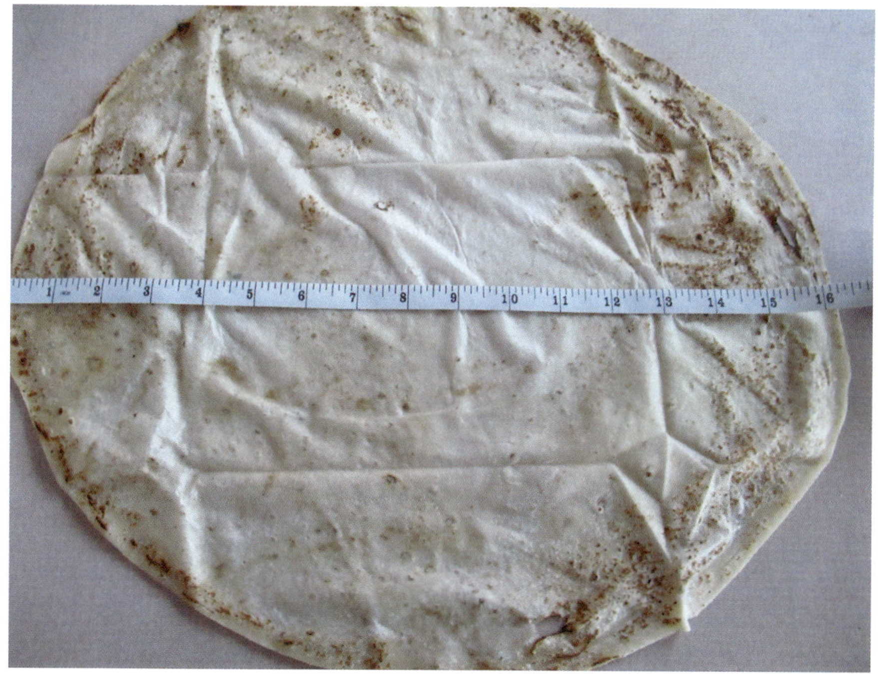

The biggest tortillas make the biggest chimichangas. *Author photo.*

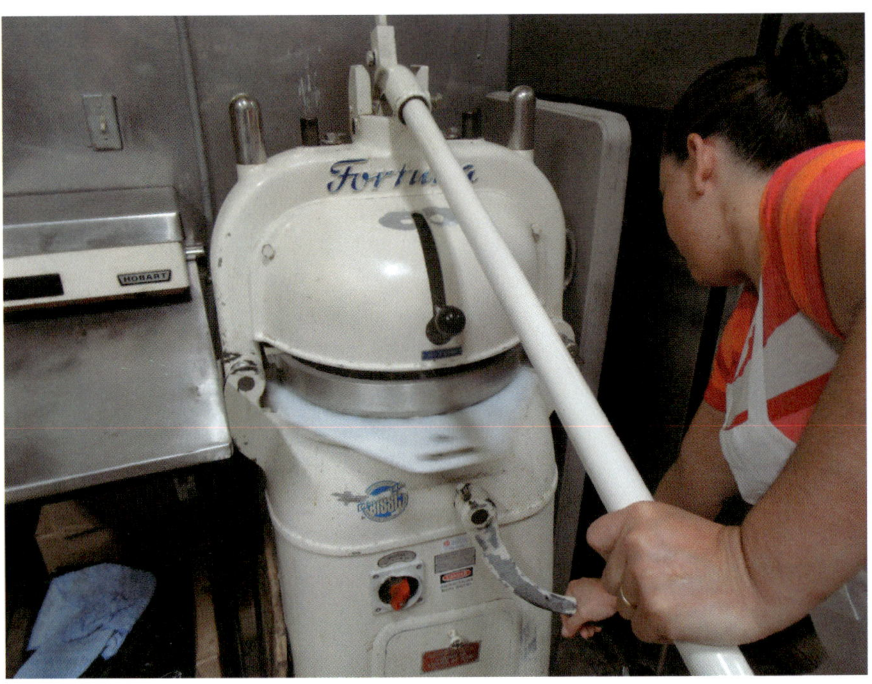

The dough is put in the press machine to create equal-sized balls of tortilla dough, *Author photo.*

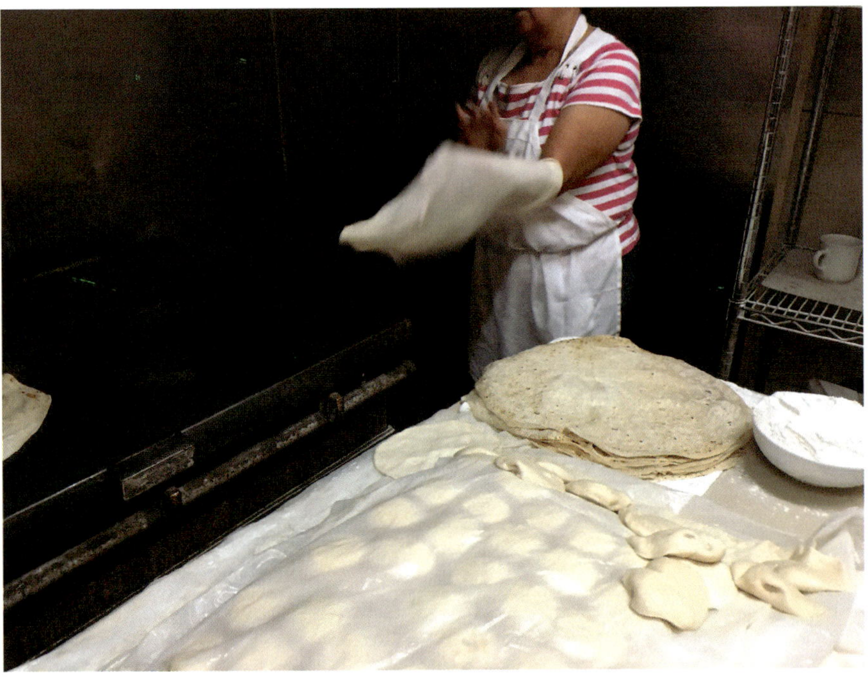

The tortillas are flipped back and forth as they are stretched paper thin. *Author photo.*

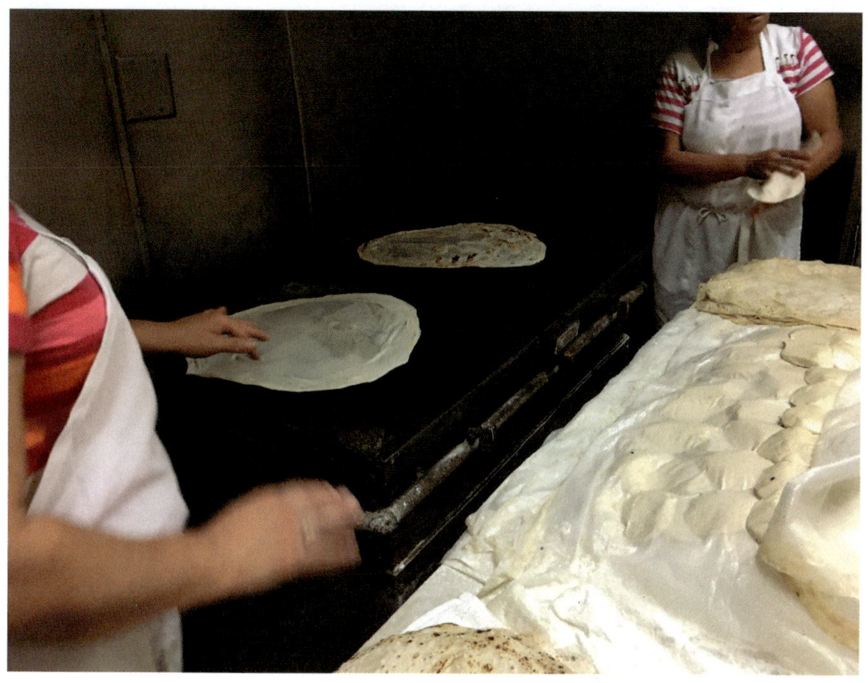

The team works in perfect unison to create hundreds of tortillas every day. *Author photo.*

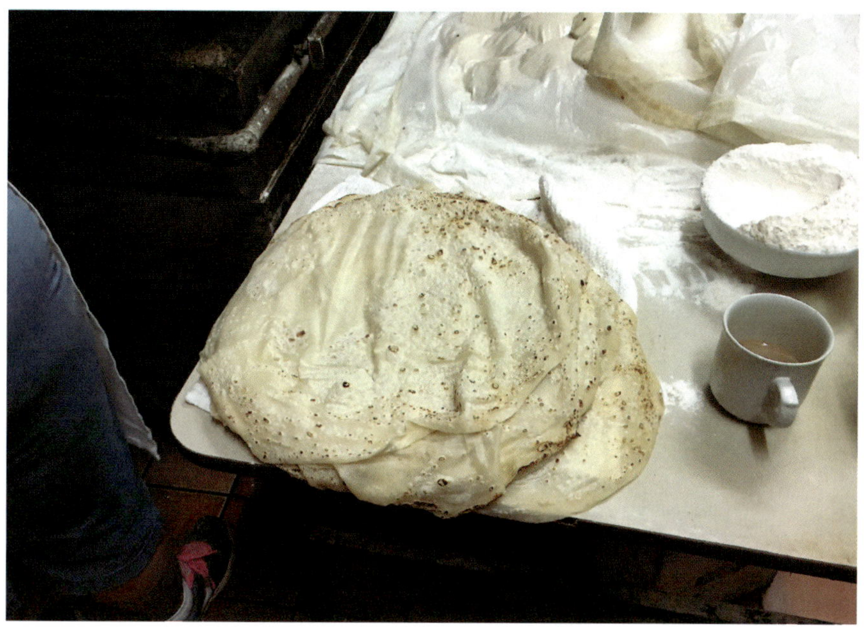

The final product: a stack of warm, soft tortillas. *Author photo.*

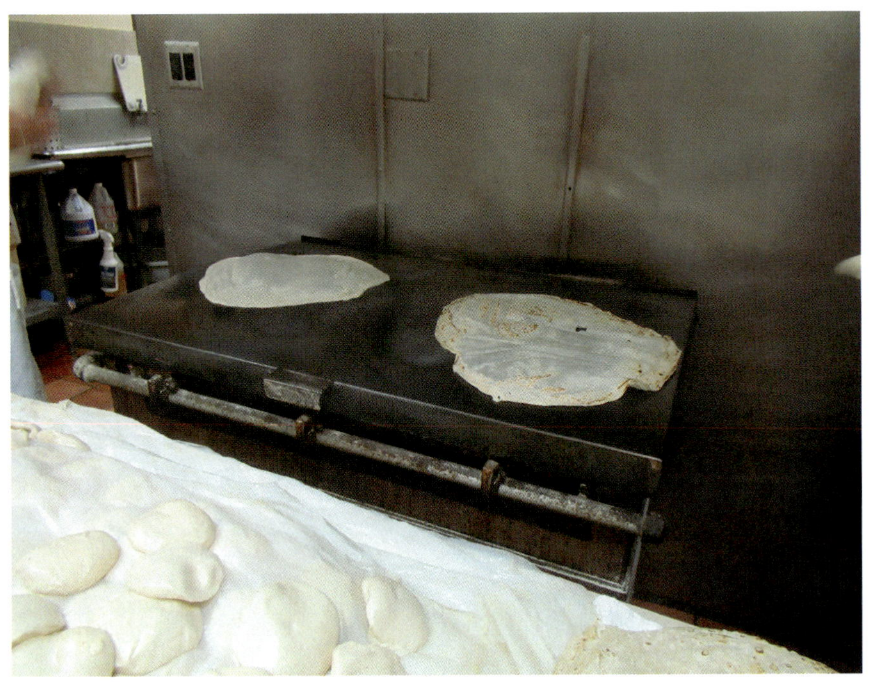

The griddle was made just to cook tortillas. *Author photo.*

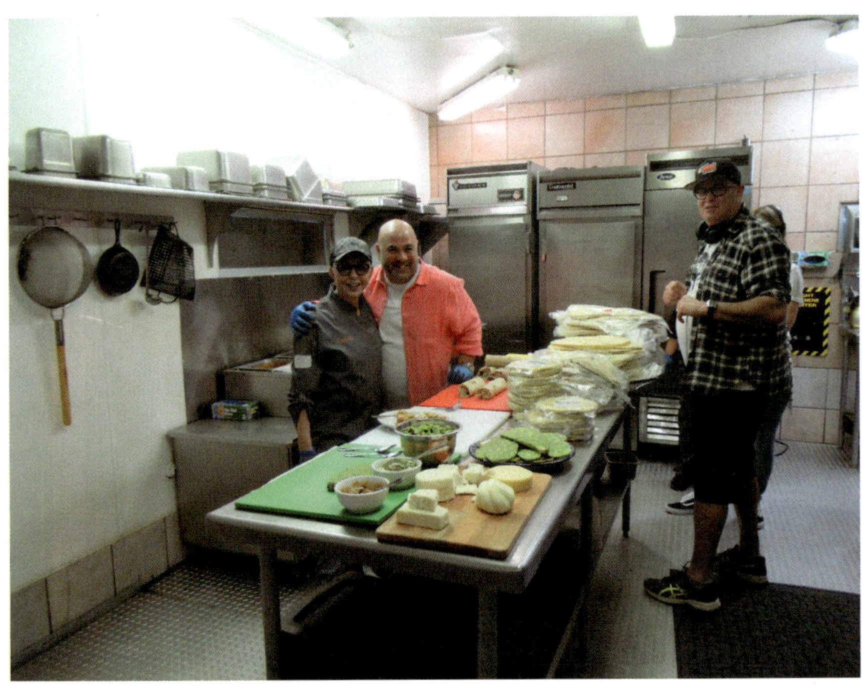

In the kitchen with Carlotta Flores and Frankie Olivieri from Pat's King of Steaks. *Author photo.*

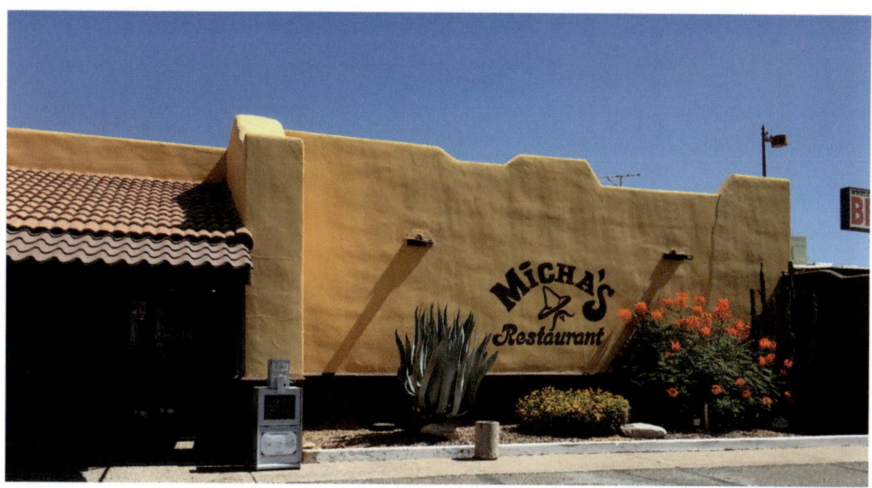

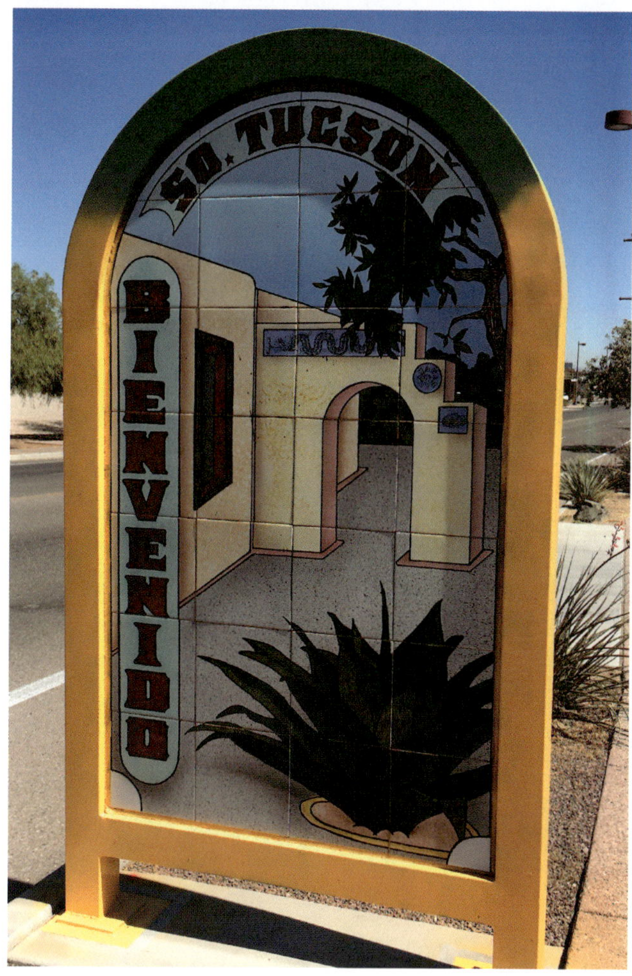

Above: Micha's before the fire. *Author photo*.

Right: Welcome to south Tucson, where chimichangas are plentiful and delicious. *Author photo*.

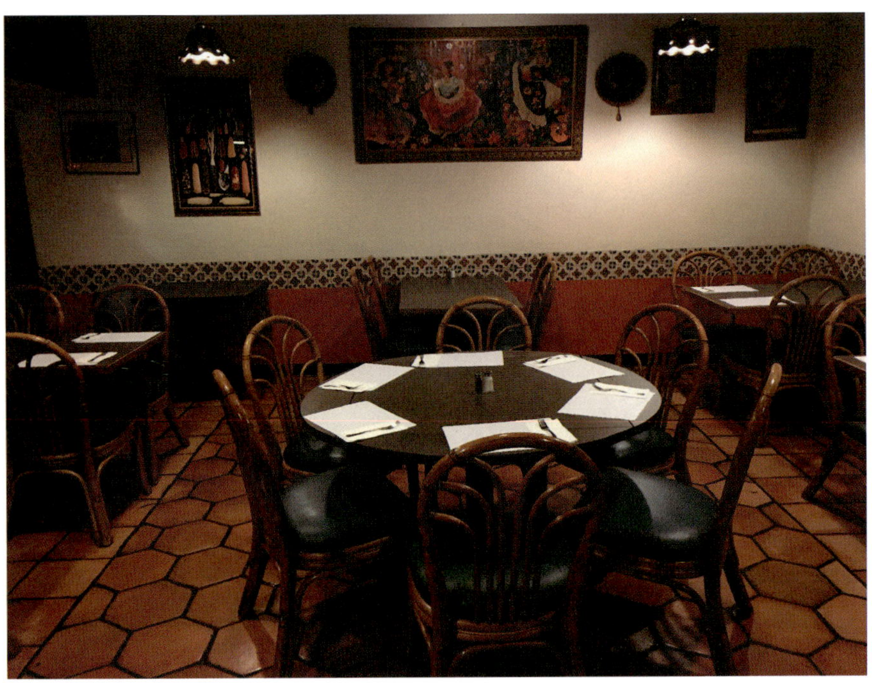

One of several dining rooms at Micha's. *Author photo.*

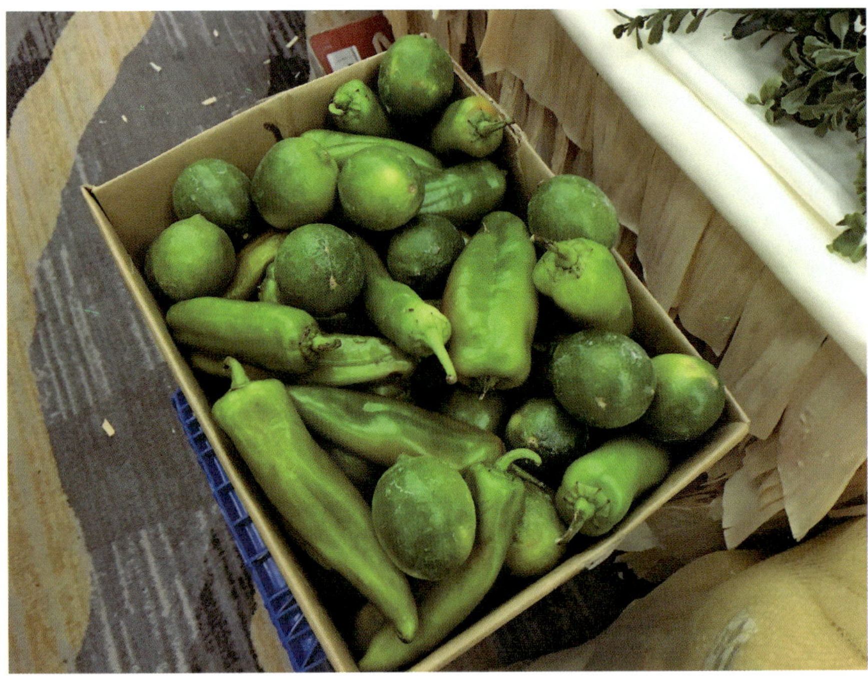

A box of chiles ready for roasting. *Author photo.*

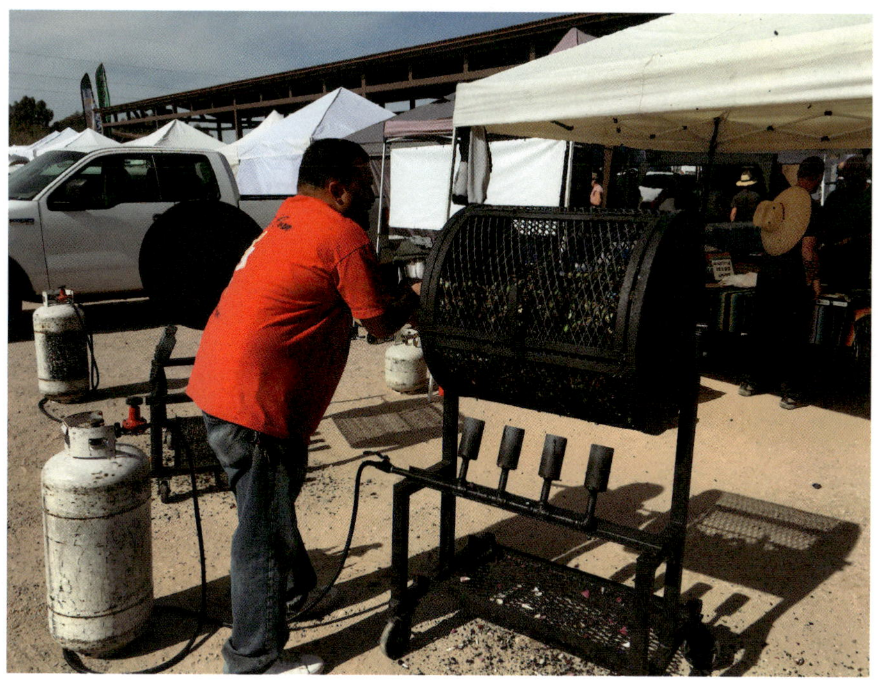

Roasting chiles the traditional way. *Author photo*.

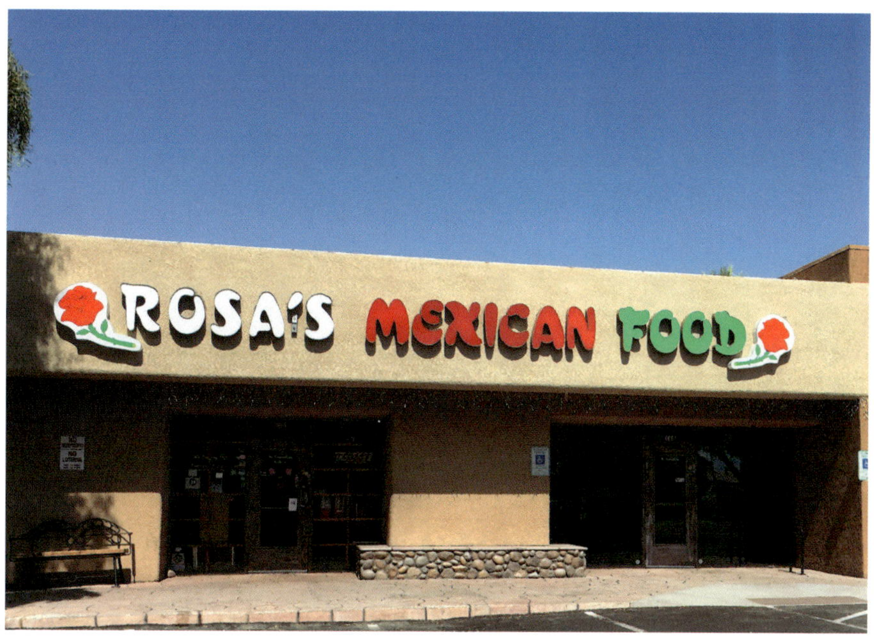

Rosa's Mexican Food is now in its third generation. *Author photo*.

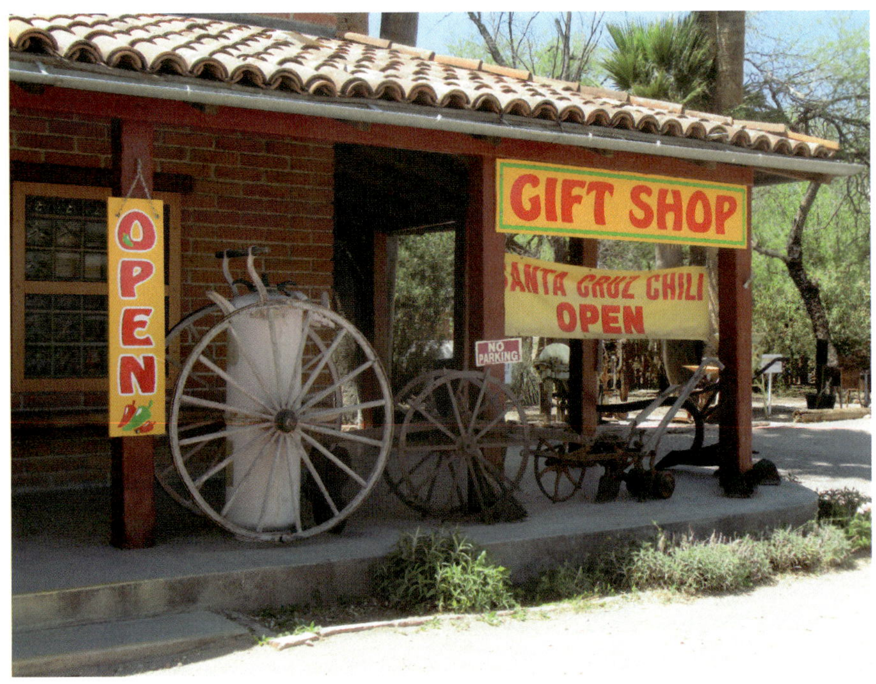

You can get your supplies at Santa Cruz Chili and Spice Company in Tumacacori. *Author photo.*

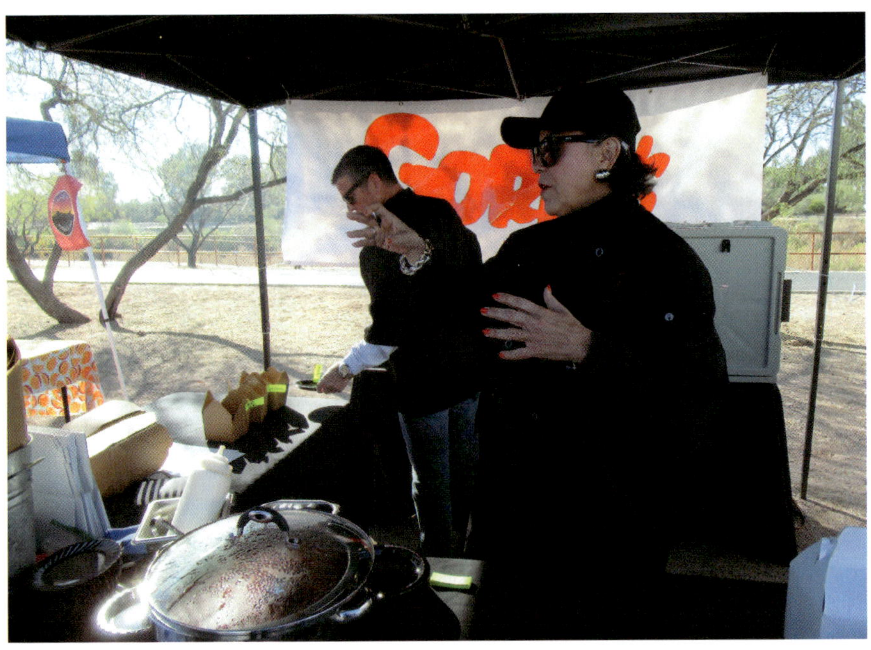

Marguerite and Mark at Gordo's 2.0 booth at the Heirloom Farmers' Market. *Author photo.*

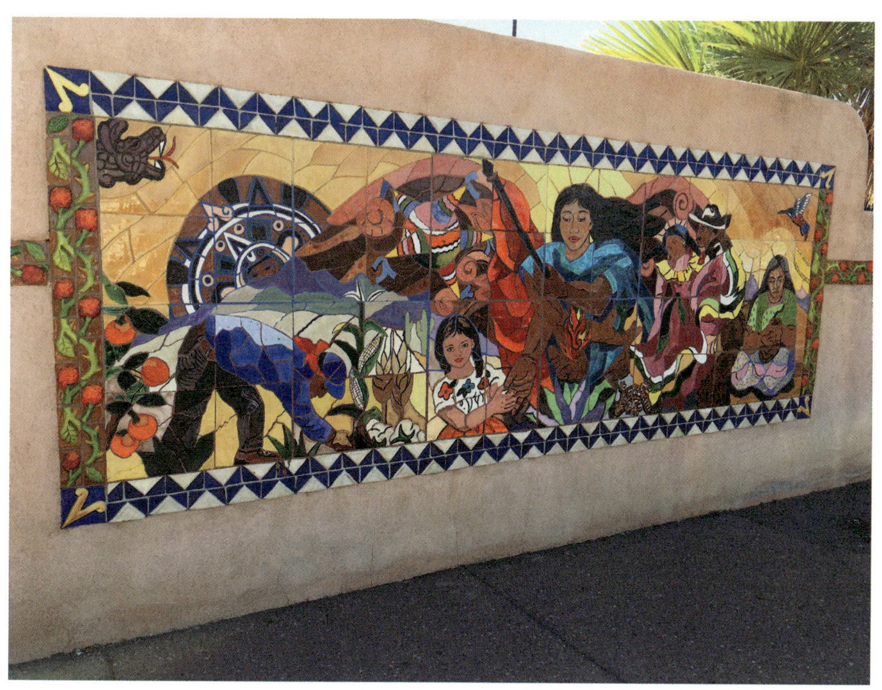

Murals like this beauty are found all over Tucson. *Author photo.*

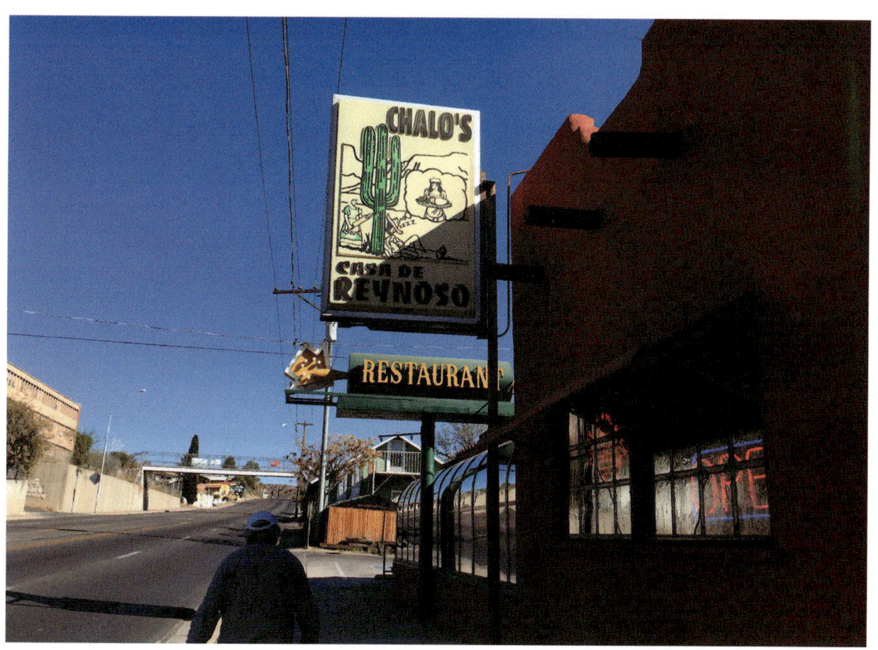

Chalo's Casa de Reynoso in Globe. *Author photo.*

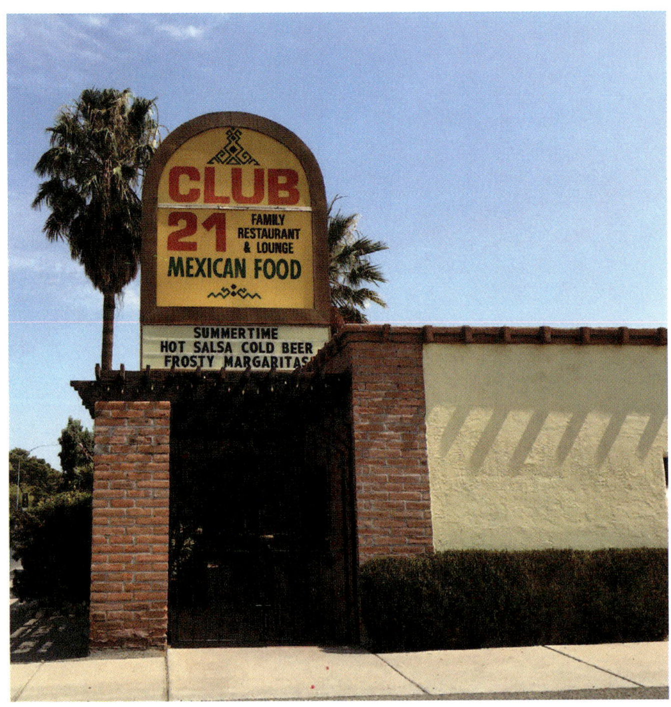

Left: Club 21 is one of Tucson's oldest Mexican restaurants. *Author photo*.

Below: The dining room at Mi Patio in Phoenix. *Author photo*.

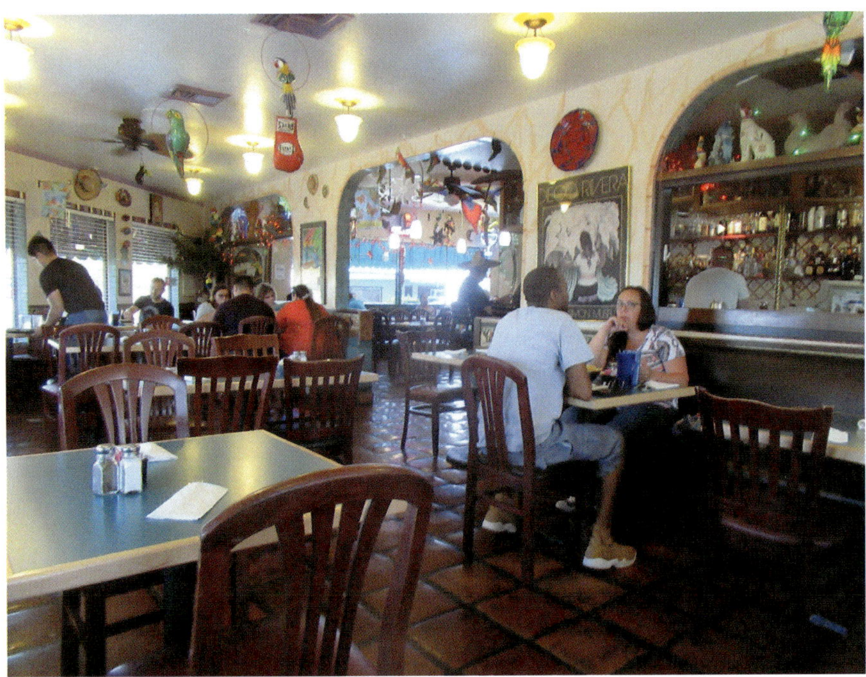

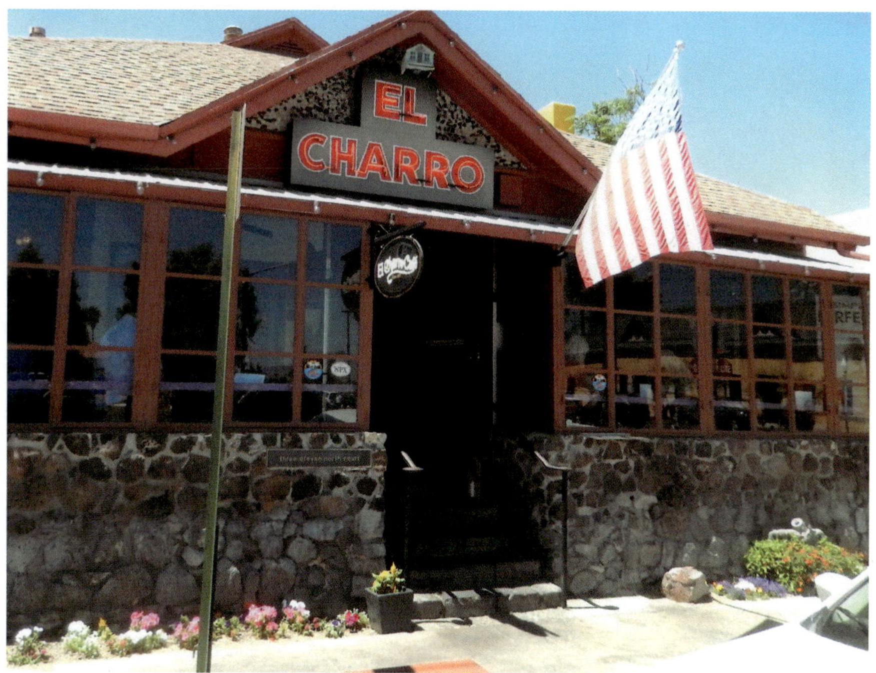

El Charro is a culinary icon. *Author photo.*

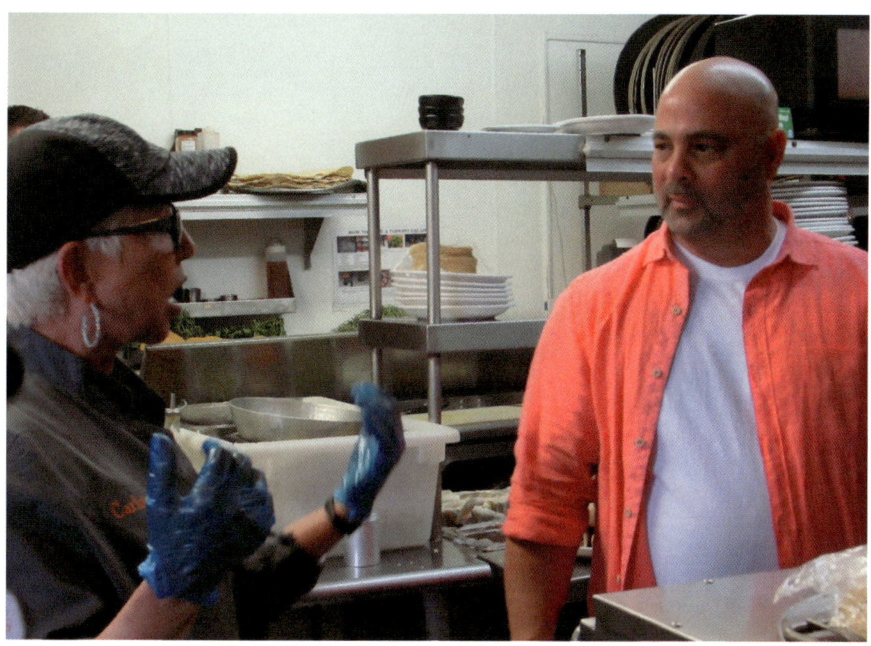

Carlotta Flores and Frankie Olivieri of Pat's King of Steaks discussing the history of chimichangas and cheesesteaks. *Author photo.*

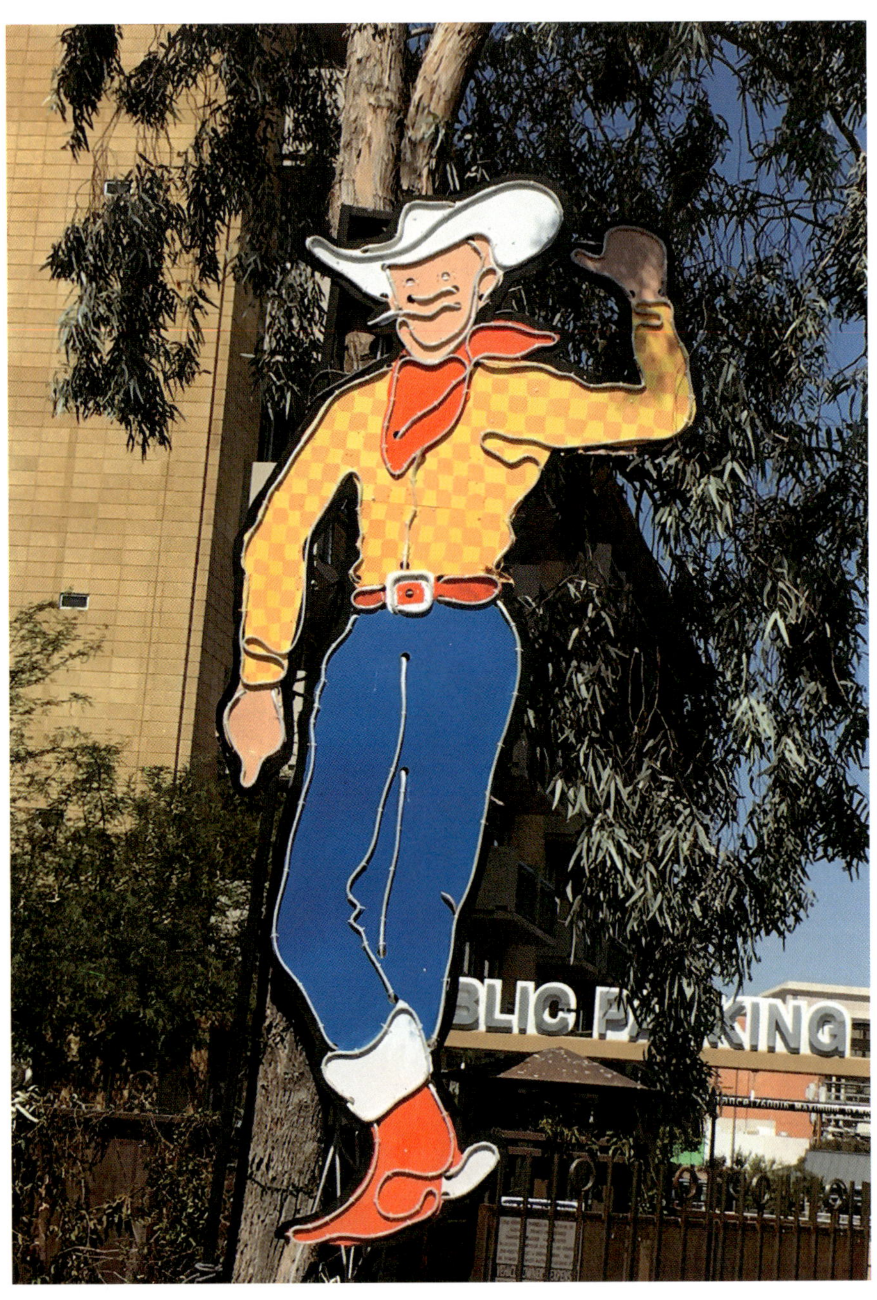

Howdy from Arizona! Home of so many chimichangas. *Author photo.*

CAROLINA'S MEXICAN FOOD

Food writers seldom wax rhapsodic when describing their experiences, especially when it comes to humble little places like Carolina's (pronounced like the state) in South Phoenix. But when phrases like "the best chimi I've ever had," "shattering crisp" and "the tortilla is like a cloud" pop out from the mouths of professional food writers, then you know there's something special going on at Carolina's. Others agree, as Carolina's has won numerous "Best of's" year after year.

Carolina's Mexican Food opened in 1968 in a place just slightly bigger than a closet. But after having spent years selling burros, tacos and tamales out of the trunk of their car, Carolina Valenzuela and her husband, Manuel, felt like they were in heaven.

This was a family affair. Carolina's mom, Elvira Castellanos de Avril, the originator of many of the recipes, worked alongside her daughter in the kitchen for bingo money. Their son, Edward, washed dishes. Manuel ran the front of the house. Longtime fans of the makeshift kitchen were

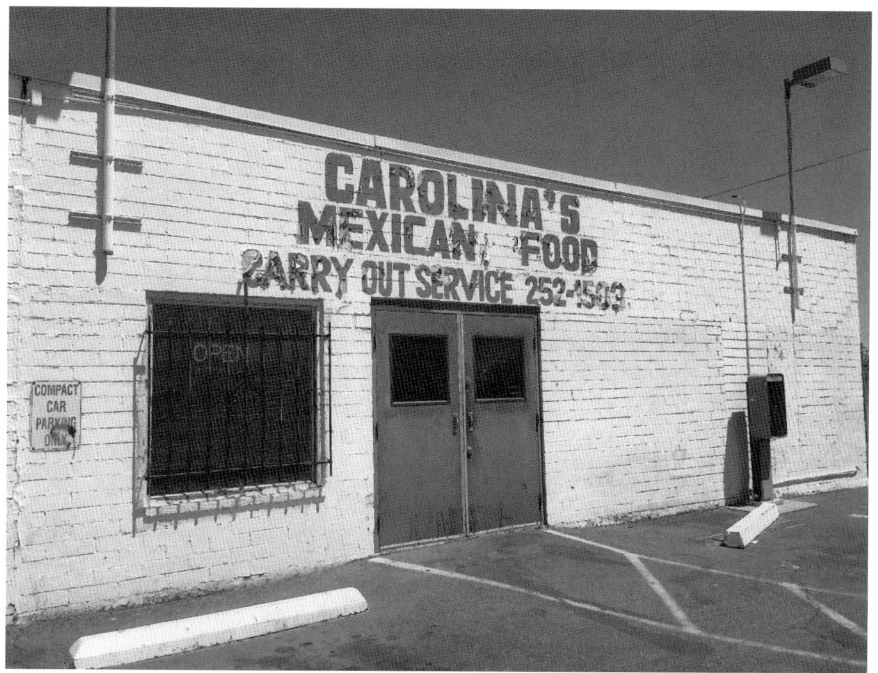

The legendary Carolina's. *Author photo.*

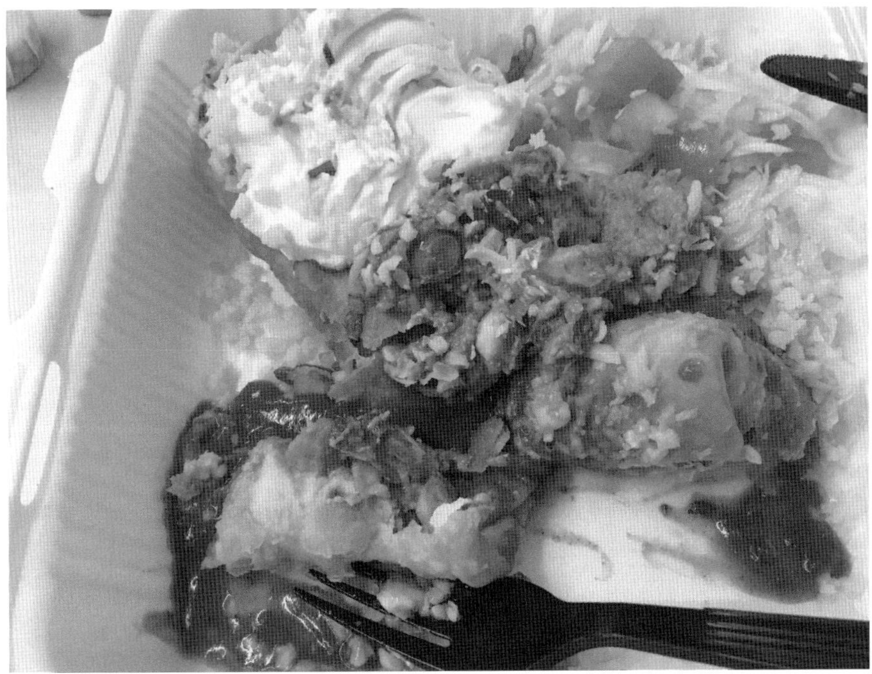

This red chili chimi is found at Carolina's. *Author photo.*

thrilled that they could find their favorites in a permanent building, and the business blossomed.

In 1972, they moved to a larger place on Mohave Street. Manny died in 1979, and Carolina and the family carried on. Then, when the city needed the property for the new Sky Harbor Airport, they moved the restaurant again, just down the street. This was in 1986, and by this time, son Joe was involved in the business.

Carolina was still actively involved, but Edward, Joe and his wife, Phyllis, did everything from hiring and firing to running the catering department, with their mom presiding over it all. Edward retired sometime in the early 1990s, and then in 1998, Joe suffered a major heart attack. Fortunately, the grandchildren stepped in, and Carolina's continued serving their famous food. Josephine Quinones and her husband, Oscar, were there, as were other grands, Victoria Tiendens and Angela and Jennifer Hernandez. Today, the restaurant is run by Victoria and her husband, David. Carolina died in 2002.

Inside, folks order at the counter and then take a seat at one of the many mismatched Formica topped tables in an attached room. Everything is served in Styrofoam containers, and the to-go orders are as numerous as the eat-in orders. The soda fountain contains such options as horchata and jamaica in addition to a dozen popular soft drinks. Families, construction workers, groups of friends and elderly couples fill the tables and eat, and because service is quick and the atmosphere barebones, they are out in a flash. The place is noisy, but no one seems to mind.

The menu lists numerous options for burros: beans, beans with potatoes, chorizo, chorizo with beans or potatoes, red chile, green chile, red machaca, green machaca, red chicken, green chicken, chicken with beans and several combinations. And here is where it gets complicated. For an additional cost ($1.65), you can have any of the burros "deep-fried to a golden crisp."

There is one chimichanga, but apparently the difference between a deep-fried burro and a chimi at Carolina's is the addition of guacamole and sour cream on top with beans and rice on the side. You can have any burro served this way.

What makes the chimis at Carolina's stand out are the tortillas. An army of cooks rolls, pats and griddles the giant, soft flour tortillas that are made fresh

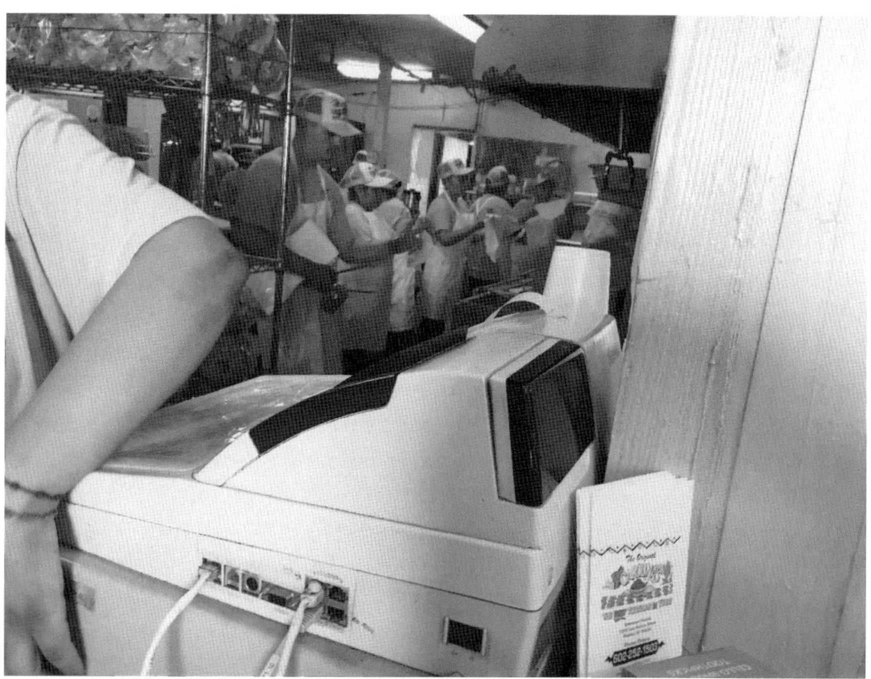

A typical day at Carolina's. *Author photo.*

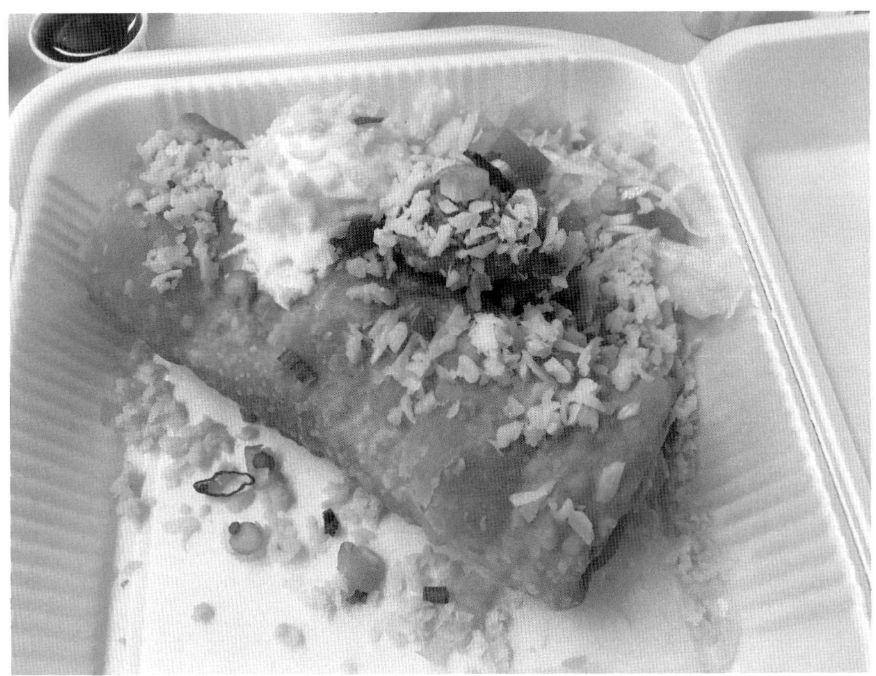

Carolina's superb chimis are all served in Styrofoam. *Author photo.*

to order. Fifteen inches in diameter, paper thin and with a slight chewiness, Carolina's makes four hundred to five hundred tortillas per day, every day. The warm tortillas are available to take home—if they make it that far, as the aroma is irresistible.

Once a tortilla is transformed into a chimi, the outside is crisp and crackly; inside, the tortilla retains an airy tenderness that stands up to whatever filling there might be. The red chili is rich with big chunks of beef in a red sauce with a low heat. The green chili is savory and lightly spicy. The shredded beef is tender and juicy. All in all, it's a remarkable chimichanga.

Today, there are four slightly more upscale Carolina's sites spread throughout the Valley (they are run by Carolina's granddaughters and are a separate company), but the heart and soul of Carolina's is still at the white block building in South Phoenix.

A trip to the South Phoenix Carolina's may seem a bit out of the way just to eat a chimichanga, but once you cut in to the crispy, crackling shell and take a bite of the savory filling, one realizes that a Carolina's chimi is one of the best in the Valley.

LA PINATA

La Pinata has another claim on chimichangas, but they aren't saying they created it. Chef and owner Peter Bugarin Jr. tells this story of his contribution to the chimi story: "I got out of the navy in 1970, and I was going to be a physician. I started working for the Garcia family [of the now national chain Garcia's Mexican Restaurants]. And I liked it very much. About a year later, we opened the restaurant, and we've been in business for forty-eight years," he said.

"The Garcias were very kind to me and very encouraging. Olivia showed me as much as she could, and when I opened the restaurant, my mother [Esperanza] helped me a lot. My father [Peter Sr.] was the business brains," Bugarin added. But as it usually is with creative people with a passion, he wanted to do things his way.

"They had a chimi there, back then it was just a deep-fried burro with sour cream on top, so when I opened my restaurant and got my first order of chimichangas, I panicked. I put guacamole in the center and sour cream on each end and tomatoes and onions and cheese and an olive....It got the tag 'the Mexican Version of the Banana Split' [because of the big scoops of goodies on top]. And that's my claim to fame," he said with a laugh.

In those early years, La Pinata developed a reputation for making great Sonoran food. The whole family—Peter, his parents, his four sisters and an aunt—were all involved in the restaurant, but eventually the usual family squabbles resulted in an expansion.

His father, who had been a famous bandleader and musician in the Phoenix area, made sure that each child had his or her own restaurant, so there were five versions of La Pinata scattered throughout the Valley for a time. Things went well for a while, but then the family realized that they weren't able to spend the time together, time that was important to all of them. Eventually, all but the original closed. Two sisters went back to teaching. Ramona and Roseanne took over duties at the restaurant. Roseanne now runs the front of the house, while Ramona does the books.

Peter Sr. died in 2003, and the family wasn't sure how Ezperanza would survive without the man she had been married to for decades. "He protected her," said Bugarin. "She was his queen." The family found some peace in the fact that their father passed just as he was beginning to not recognize his queen and they were concerned for her well-being.

But Ezperanza surprised everyone by coming out of her shell. "She blossomed," her son said commenting on his mom's sense of humor and

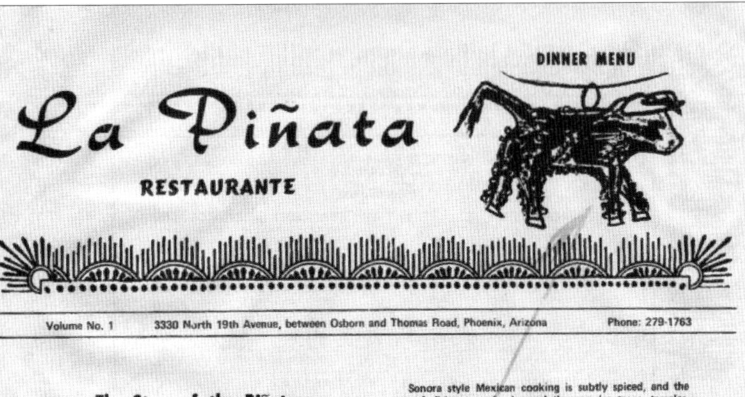

DINNER MENU

La Piñata

RESTAURANTE

Volume No. 1 — 3330 North 19th Avenue, between Osborn and Thomas Road, Phoenix, Arizona — Phone: 279-1763

The Story of the Piñata

Originally the Piñata was only a part of the Mexican Christmas festivities. Its origin dates back many centuries, even before the arrival of the Spanish Conquistadors on Mexican soil.

The Mexican Indians fashioned the Piñata from a fragile earthen jar made especially to hold simple toys and favors. They were gaily decorated; some to look like the gods they worshipped, others to symbolize events, etc.

The Piñata soon gained favor with the early Spanish explorers and they began sending them to their mother lands of Spain and Portugal.

The Piñata was then on its way to becoming an international sign of "Fiesta".

Today the children of Mexico, and millions more like them throughout the world, follow the tradition started by their ancestors.

They form a circle around a Piñata, which is hung from the ceiling, and put one of their number in the center with his eyes blindfolded. He is given a stick and permitted three tries at breaking it. The other children, meanwhile, sing and dance around in a circle. If the first child does not succeed in breaking the jar, another child tries. When the Piñata is broken, causing a shower of gifts to pour down onto the floor, the entire party makes a wild scramble to obtain their share.

Sometimes three Piñatas are hung in the room. One is filled with water; another with confetti; another with gifts, sweets and goodies - this is the good Piñata.

La Piñata is a symbol of all the good that is to come. We hope that La Piñata Restaurante will be your symbol of good Mexican food and that you will come often.

Tell your friends to come and read our story of the Piñata.

About Our Food

Mexican cuisine dates back many centuries to the ancient Aztec, then later Spanish and French influences. To the Spanish conquistadors, the native cuisine of the Aztecs came as a delight, making use of foods then unknown outside of the Americas, such as chocolate, vanilla, corn, chiles, peanuts, tomatoes, avocados, squash, beans, pineapple and papaya. Spain added oil, wine, cinnamon, cloves, rice, wheat, and the cattle provided beef, milk, and butter. Later during the brief reign of Maximilian and Carlotta, more sophisticated dishes of French, Austrian, and Italian origin were introduced.

Sonora style Mexican cooking is subtly spiced, and the range of dishes goes far beyond the popular tacos, tamales, and enchiladas. Mexican food need not be peppery, although for those desiring added pepperiness we have spicy table sauce.

We feel it important that not only should our food taste well, but that the food we buy be the best available. We spend that extra time and money to insure that our chef, José has the best produce, best aged Prime and Choice meats, and best ingredients available with which to prepare your meal.

Mexican Kitchen Talk

Taco: A crisp tortilla stuffed with meat and shredded lettuce, topped with grated cheese and diced tomatoes.

Enchilada: A tortilla dipped in chili sauce stuffed with cheese and onions, or meat, rolled and topped with more cheese, sauce and onions.

Tamale: Tasty meat and red chile wrapped in corn husks, which has been spread with "corn masa" then cooked in steam.

Chili Relleno: Selected green chili, stuffed with cheese, dipped in egg batter, and deep fried to a golden brown.

Tostada: A crisp tortilla with refried beans, melted cheese, lettuce and tomato.

Tortilla: Thin pancake-like bread, of corn or white flour. Main ingredient of tacos or enchiladas.

Chimichanga: Deep fried meat burro topped with sour cream, and guacamole garnish.

Flauta: Tasty meat wrapped in corn tortilla, deep fried and garnished with guacamole.

Please enjoy our restaurant. Smile, laugh, smile some more. Eat, drink, and eat some more. Start a contest of wits, or just stare dreamily at each other. Be Happy if you feel happy; Loving if you feel loving. It's your evening, we'll do all we can to make it exciting.¡Con Mucho Gusto!

From all of us at La Piñata,

Your Host,

Pete Bugarin

Pete Bugarin

La Pinata's menu. *Courtesy of La Pinata.*

newfound independence. "She was one of the funniest people I ever knew," he said. Ezperanza died in 2014.

In 2015, La Pinata moved into a smaller place, taking the famous neon sign with it. A chef who started at the restaurant in the kitchen in 1978 also made the move and he is still there. "The kitchen is a third of the size of the old place," Bugarin said. And with the move, he decided to change the menu to make it more "modern."

"In the first three months, we changed the menu five times," Bugarin said. But those changes didn't sit right with the customers who followed Bugarin to the new site. They told him, "No, we want what you've been doing for forty-five years." And so, they returned to their roots, serving what the people wanted.

There have been certain menu concessions to the way people eat, and new chimis are on the menu. "We have carnitas," Bugarin said. "And the shrimp chimi." There are also mini-chimis on the appetizer menu. "We've been in business for forty-eight years, serving the same Sonoran food that made us successful." He noted with a smile in his voice, "We hope to be in business for another forty-eight."

In 2018, as part of Orbitz's "Ultimate Foodie Road Trip," La Pinata's chimichanga was the Arizona choice.

AUNT CHILADA'S

The long and colorful history of Aunt Chilada's at Squaw Peak begins before Arizona became a state. Over the decades, the space has been home to numerous entities, all of which were gathering spots of some kind.

From about 1890 through 1935, the spot was a general store and trading post where the miners from the nearby mercury mines could head for supplies and refreshments. The work affected the men in unusual ways because mercury is toxic and over time can cause neurological damage. Short term effects, however, for the miners caused them to seem high and dreamy-eyed. The pass that they came down to get to the general store was thus named Dreamy Draw, the name of the road where Aunt Chilada's is located.

The owners at the time of the end of Prohibition were Jesse and Dave Noble, who applied and got the first post-Prohibition liquor license in Arizona. Shortly thereafter, the site became the Peak Steakhouse. But steaks really weren't what attracted people. Above the area that is now the

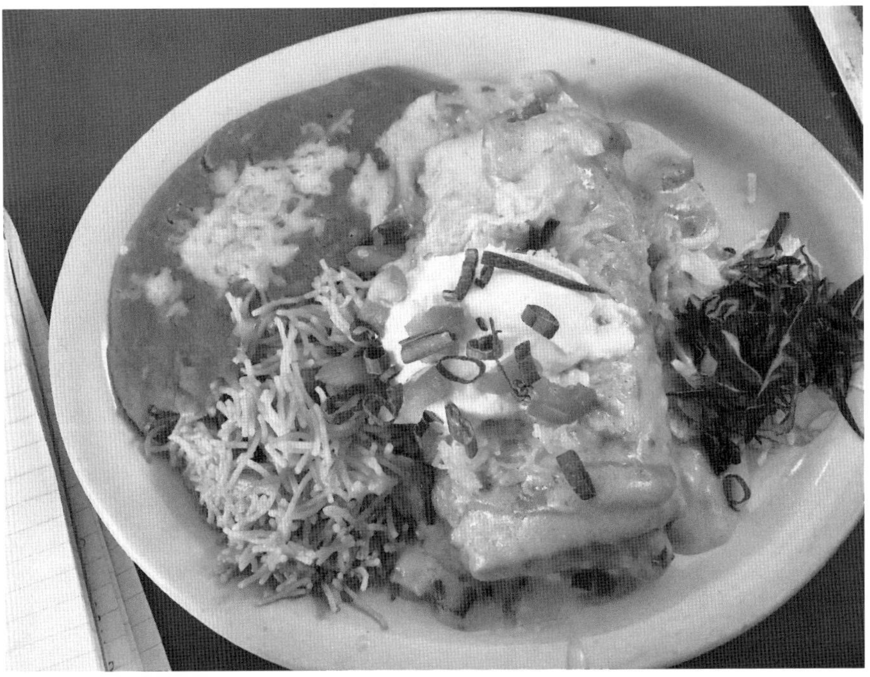

The seafood chimi from Aunt Chilada's. *Author photo.*

bar, there was a large windowed space where young women would dance and cavort in a provocative manner. Needless to say, the steakhouse was immensely popular.

The next incarnation was George's Olé, a Mexican restaurant. George Cocherham added several rooms to the restaurant with the help of his coworkers, firefighters from the Phoenix Fire Department. The firefighters hauled and set three thousand railroad ties from the once busy Santa Fe Railroad and tons and tons of river rock to build the additional rooms. Today, the ties and rocks are still in place and add a charming, rustic look to Aunt Chilada's.

George served barbecued meats, and as one story goes, chimichangas were also on the menu. There's no proof of that claim, but then again, there's no proof he didn't.

The name Aunt Chilada's came about in the 1980s with another ownership change. By this time, the Pointe, a high-end resort, had been built, and Bob Gosnell bought the restaurant. His friend and co-worker Ken Nagel, who was instrumental in all aspects of the resort from its beginnings to a vast network of dining options, then bought the restaurant with partner Lee Midtun in 1995.

Today, the Nagel family—Ken, Candice and daughters Tiffany Allison, Michele Woods, Tami Butcher and Jenni Jefferies O'Brien—run Aunt Chilada's and have created a fabulous meeting spot for the posh neighborhood of homes and condos that have sprung up around it. There isn't a day of the week where an event or three doesn't take place there. Weddings, baby showers, bachelor parties, family reunions and more are all a big part of Aunt Chilada's, and with six hundred seats, the restaurant can still serve regular customers while huge private parties take place in banquet rooms. One of the banquet rooms was converted from the original stable of the general store. "We're a landmark destination," said Tiffany, who is a chef and de facto spokesperson at the restaurant.

The menu is large and diverse, with items made from only the best ingredients. Both traditional food and creative takes, such as the wood-fired Mexican pizza and Mexican hot dogs, are served. Tiffany proudly talks about her dad being a stickler for not cutting corners even if that means it will cost a little more.

The menu lists only one chimi, but any burro can be prepared as a chimi. There are Burritos Classico with bean, vegetable, green chili, red chili, chicken, picadillo, machaca, carne asada and carnitas, and then there are the especiales.

The fajita has grilled beef or chicken with tomatoes, onions and poblano peppers. The chicken pechuga has grilled chicken and is served enchilada style with Mexican cheese sauce. The spinach and chicken chimi is topped with provolone cheese. And then there's the seafood chimi/burro that is filled with perfectly seasoned grilled shrimp and scallops and finished off with the same rich, cheesy sauce found on the pechuga chimis. All are served with beans and fideo, a thin pasta similar to pilaf, cooked in tomato sauce.

An appetizer that Aunt Chilada's calls "chingalingas" is another take on chimis. Here a flour tortilla is filled with either machaca or chicken and then rolled tightly much like a flauta and served with either enchilada or barbecue sauce.

The vibe here is one of fun and good times, but families, dates and small groups will feel at home in any of the rooms or gorgeous patios. "Our bar customers think it's a bar, and our restaurant customers think it's a restaurant," Tiffany said.

One regular customer is a ghost. "She's the wife of the guy who ran the railroad station that was nearby," said Michele. "She hung herself. I've never

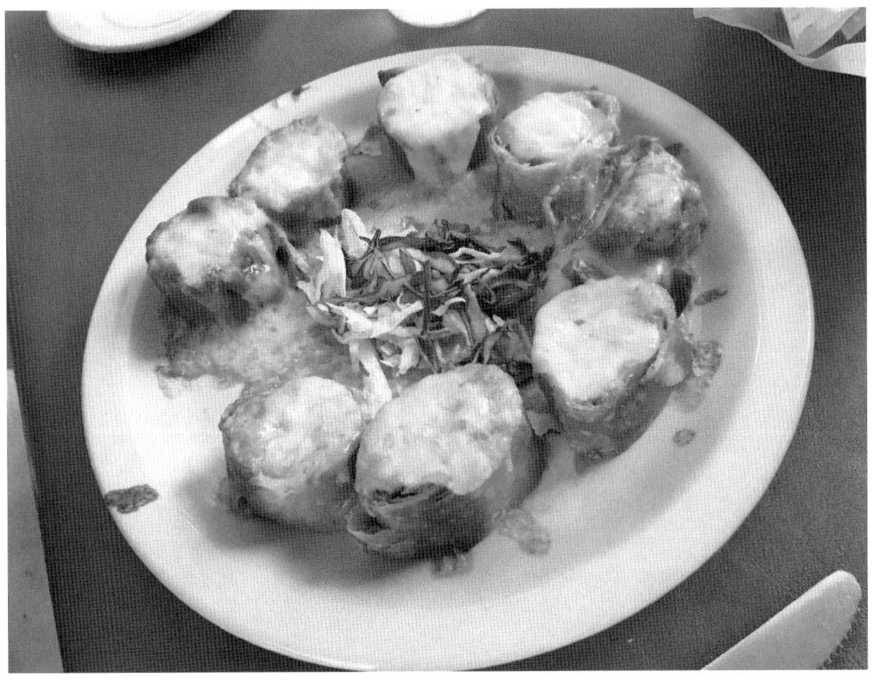

Chingalingas from Aunt Chilada's. *Author photo.*

seen her." But she added that paranormal professionals have come in and attested to the presence of a young woman all dressed in white.

There is another Aunt Chilada's in Tempe that is not associated with the original.

Eight generations of several families have created a long history at this valley favorite. Aunt Chilada's is a modern eatery that honors and celebrates the colorful past, from dreamy-eyed miners to first-rate barbecue to chimichangas with a twist.

LOS DOS MOLINOS

The food at Los Dos Molinos isn't quite like most of the other Mexican food found in the Valley. Instead of the Sonoran fare, the food at Los Dos has its roots in New Mexico, and that means heat—hot, lip-burning, tear-inducing heat from lots and lots of chiles.

You'll find many of the same dishes found elsewhere, but instead of the mild laid-back flavors found in Sonoran cooking, New Mexican fare is infused with fire.

And Los Dos Molinos is known to serve some of the fieriest food around. In fact, it's been called the "Hottest Food in Phoenix" by the *Phoenix New Times*.

Victoria Chavez, who opened the first Los Dos in the 1970s, moved to Arizona as a child from New Mexico when her dad, who worked for the U.S. Forest Service, was transferred to Springerville. In high school, she met Eddie Chavez, the love of her life. Together, they would raise five children (Sandy, Loretta, Anthony, Cheryl and Antoinette), run a self-supporting ranch, sustain tragedy and create a restaurant empire that taught Arizonans what New Mexican food is all about.

The inspiration for a restaurant began when a friend asked Victoria to cook her homemade food at his mountain resort. From there, she persuaded Eddie to build her a simple A-frame where she could sell tacos. There were six tables.

The name Los Dos Molinos translates to "the Two Mills," in this case two family heirlooms. One mill had belonged to Eddie's family in St. John's, a small town not far from Springerville. The second mill was handed down to Victoria from her great-grandmother. Both had been used daily by the families, so Victoria and Eddie felt that Los Dos Molinos was a most fitting name for their tiny spot.

In 1977, a larger, full-service restaurant followed, and by the time her children were grown and grandchildren were running around, five Los Dos Molinos could be found in Phoenix, Mesa and Springerville.

The Mesa restaurant has a story all to itself. Victoria had noticed a run-down old building on her travels between the restaurant and home, and she knew she had to have it for her next venture—never mind the fact that the interior was damaged by fire, windows were smashed out and the ceiling leaked in numerous places. It was in such bad condition that the city was preparing to tear it down.

In previous incarnations, the site had been the ranch of silent film cowboy star Tom Mix, a commune and a funeral home. In the movie *Una Dia de Vez* (*One Day at a Time*), Victoria told how she went to the bank and took out a loan without Eddie knowing. She also related the relief she felt when she didn't get the winning bid and the fear she had when the sellers called and told her the place was hers because the first buyer backed out. Victoria also noted that she paid the loan off in six months. That was in 1989.

The film chronicles the story of the Los Dos Molinos empire and the Chavez family. Her grandson Drew Melton produced the film in honor of his grandmother, saying during an interview in the film, "Gramma built this beautiful thing for all of us."

In the movie, you get glimpses of the EA Ranch, which Eddie and Victoria built themselves and where they raised their family. You see the interior of the various restaurants with all the kitschy décor and bright colors. Some might not appreciate the mishmash of items (license plates, chiles, kachina dolls, tools, cowboy hats, beer bottle chandeliers and more), but each item is part of the Chavez family story.

Certain themes run throughout the film and give a hint as to why Los Dos Molinos has been so successful. One is respect. The Chavez children were taught to respect their parents, their siblings and customers. Cheryl talks about how that respect helped the family get along through good times and bad.

Another theme, which every member of the family mentions, is hard work. From the time they were little, the children were given responsibilities on the ranch and at the restaurants. They saw how their parents worked together, whether it was building a wall or managing multiple restaurants. All noted that even though some might consider the family poor, the kids were never left wanting for anything.

The third theme, although it isn't really spoken, is love of family. Victoria and Eddie were married for fifty-four years until Eddie died in 2005 due to complications from a brain injury he'd sustained in a motorcycle accident. The love sustained them through the deaths of Anthony in 1977 at the age of eighteen and Loretta several years later—both died in vehicle accidents. The love and support were there when Sandy moved to New York and opened a Los Dos Molinos in Manhattan and also when she returned home. The love kept them together as they declared bankruptcy with the newest restaurant in Ahwatukee (opened in 2011 and closed in 2017) and, most recently, when they decided to close the original restaurant in Springerville in 2018.

Today, the three remaining Los Dos Molinos attract customers from all over the Valley. They come for the eye-popping, tongue-singeing dishes that Victoria created. All the chiles used come from New Mexico and are roasted and peeled by hand. They buy more than twenty sacks every year. And the chiles go into everything.

Customers are fully warned from the minute they open their menus, with the heat levels marked for each dish. There's also a note on the menu that states, "Food is spicy. You order it, you own it." Even the salsa takes the heat level to the stratosphere, but again, diners can't say they weren't warned. A sign tells everyone, "I am sorry we do not provide a mild salsa. I do not know how to make mild."

The signature adovada pork ribs, the ones that Bobby Flay raved about when he featured Los Dos on his Food Network show, are a big draw, as are the New Mexico–style enchiladas with a fried egg on top.

On the menu, people can order a deep-fried burro or go all out and order a chimichanga, which comes with sour cream and guacamole and is smothered in either Hatch New Mexican red sauce or the spicy green chili. Beans and rice accompany any chimi ordered.

Chimis can be filled with the adovada or any number of other delicious options, including chicken fundido, a deep-fried burro stuffed with tender chicken and dressed in a rich sauce made with chiles and cheddar and cream cheeses. The fundido is a recipe of Victoria's nephew, John Gabaldon, who manages the Mesa restaurant. Victoria retired in 2013, and today the daughters, grandchildren and cousins are an active part in the day-to-day operations.

Every publication in the Valley has awarded Los Dos Molinos in some way, including as part of the "Best 50 Restaurants in Arizona" by both *Phoenix New Times* and *Arizona Highways*.

Valle Luna

In early 2018, *USA Today* conducted a contest to see who made the best chimichanga in Arizona as part of its "10 Best in Your State" feature. The list began with twenty statewide chimis chosen by food writers located in Phoenix, and then the readers voted on their favorites. The voting was fast and furious, with restaurant owners encouraging the vote via social media outlets. In the end, Valle Luna came out on top.

The original Valle Luna (Moon Valley) was opened in 1983 by Rita Riddle-Wilson. "Tia Rita," as she was known, had a bag full of Sonoran recipes that she had made for years at her Mexican restaurant in, of all places, Syracuse, New York, where she and her husband, Doug, had relocated to from the Valley. Tia Rita's Authentic Mexican Food was named the "Best of Syracuse Mexican Food" in spite of being a tiny, twenty-seater restaurant.

Tia learned her recipes from her friend Martha Marios. Their husbands, Doug and Pancho, had worked together at A1 Brewery in Arizona as welders, and when Pancho wanted to create a tortilla machine, Doug helped. Pancho and Martha eventually opened a highly successful tortilla chip company.

In 1983, after the dissolution of her marriage, Tia Rita returned to the Valley and opened her first Arizona restaurant on Bell Road in Phoenix. Valle Luna was so popular that another site was opened in 1985 on North Cave Creek Road. A third, larger restaurant was opened at the Boardwalk at Anderson Springs, complete with waterfront views. There was a short-lived Valle Luna in Awatukee that closed in 2005.

Rita died in 2008. Today, the restaurants are run by Tia Rita's son, Bill; his wife, Janie; and their daughters, Joey White and Reda Riddle-Bigler. The winning chimi is listed on the Tia Rita's Favorite part of the menu. "Everything we have is made with TLC," said Janie Riddle, Tia Rita's daughter-in-law. "We use fresh ingredients, no canned refried beans or anything like that," she said. "Everything is made to perfection." She noted that over the years, they've added to the menu, but most of the recipes are taken from Tia's handwritten notebook, which is part of the family inheritance.

The chimis can be filled with ground beef, shredded beef, spicy machaca, shredded chicken, red chile, green chile and, for a few dollars more, "tender, juicy, marinated" steak, pork, pollo or shrimp.

All are served with the homemade Sonoran chimi sauce. Although the recipe is a family secret, it begins as a roux, and then onions, tomatoes, tomato sauce, chiles and "lots of garlic" are added. Janie compared it to a light gravy due to the roux, although it has a thinner consistency and is also used as the relleno sauce.

Janie attributed the win to the dedication to Tia Rita's use of quality ingredients and all that TLC. She noted, "She's watching over us, and I guarantee you, if it's not right, she'll let us know," Janie said with a laugh.

No doubt with having her chimi being named "Best Chimichanga in Arizona," Tia Rita has to be smiling from above.

CASA GRANDE: SOMEWHERE BETWEEN TUCSON AND PHOENIX

Casa Grande sits at just about the halfway point between Phoenix and Tucson off I-10. Named after the nearby Casa Grande Ruins National Monument, Casa Grande has about fifty-three thousand residents, boasts a historic downtown and is home to some interesting chimis.

Anaya's Fresh Mexican Restaurant

Anaya's Fresh Mexican Food in Casa Grande (there is a second restaurant in Glendale) has a chimichanga menu with the proverbial something for everyone.

There is a Traditional chimi with either chicken or beef accompanied by lettuce, tomatoes, guacamole and sour cream. Their Arizona chimi offers a choice of chili colorado (red) or chili verde (green) with lettuce, sour cream and a double shot of guacamole.

For the more adventurous, the Seafood chimi is packed with shrimp, scallops, crab, tomatoes and onion that has been simmered in a special garlic butter sauce; the whole thing is then smothered in a chipotle sauce. Finally, the Veggie chimi has garlic-butter tossed fresh vegetables with lettuce, tomatoes, guacamole and sour cream on the side.

But then there is the Pollo Fundido, which isn't listed with the other chimis. Instead, it is found under the chicken section: "Rolled flour crispy tortilla that is filled with seasoned chicken and smothered in cream cheese sauce, garnished by sour cream and guacamole." A chimichanga by any other name….

Eva's Fine Mexican Food

Eva's first opened its doors in 1985 in a building the Cornejo family had moved to an empty lot about three miles from its original location. Opening a restaurant had been Eva's lifelong dream, and with the opening of this tiny spot, she was able to feed people from all over Casa Grande.

Later, to accommodate the crowds, the business was moved to another site, this time leaving the building behind. The new place was larger with a courtyard reminiscent of homes in Mexico. The larger space allowed Eva's son, Fernando, to add special touches turning the restaurant into a lovely, airy space.

Chimichangas can be found filled with carnitas, ground or shredded beef, red or green chili and a bean and cheese combination, but under the House Specialty heading, there is a chimi that is anything but usual. The Chimi de Mar is filled with shrimp, cod, crab and pico de gallo, and then, if that wasn't enough, Eva "smothers" (their word, not mine) the monster in her secret jalapeño cream sauce. The other chimis can be topped with any of the house sauces: Sonoran (mild red), ranchero (a medium tomato sauce with green chili), chile verde (medium green chili), tomatillo (mild but zesty) or the blanco jalapeño, which packs a little heat.

Little Sombrero

Accolades run high for this longtime Casa Grande restaurant. This tiny mom and pop shop has been called a "Casa Grande legend," "a local icon" and "a Casa Grande staple." People remember eating there on lunch break from the high school that used to be across the street more than forty years ago.

Service is from a window with picnic tables outside (there is no inside dining), but that is all part of why people love this place. Prices reflect the casual vibe. The menu on the wall doesn't list chimichangas, but for a mere $1.10, you can have any of their popular burros fried. Enchilada style is another dollar.

CENTRAL ARIZONA

Globe-Miami: The Picazo, Esparza, Reynoso Empire

Trying to keep the Reynoso/Picazo/Esparza family restaurants straight is a bit like trying to untie a Gordian knot. This family has been a part of the Globe-Miami restaurant scene since 1939, when Josefina Picazo began making and selling tamales and burros in her home. Her sisters—Pilar, Salustria and Belia—had moved back from Mexico during the Depression, and she wanted them to have the opportunities that America offered.

With barely enough money to cover the first week in business, she and her husband, Anselmo, opened a tiny restaurant on Broad Street in downtown Globe and called it El Rey. The place was tiny, barely more than a shack, but her food was so delicious and in such great demand that the restaurant allowed her to fulfill her wishes to bring her family home. Soon their children and their families were working at the restaurant in some capacity.

But the relatives were numerous, and so Josefina moved on, giving the restaurant to Salustria and Pilar. Josefina moved to Phoenix, where she opened La Paloma in 1947. Although she didn't want to, she was forced to close that place, only to open Los Compadres in 1959.

In 1971, Anselmo had a stroke and was unable to work. Daughter Lucia Valdivia offered to help until Anselmo got better; in 1971, she bought the place.

Today, her son, David, and his wife, Anna Valdivia, are in charge. They've kept the family recipes and traditions. Both Pilar's and Salustria's children

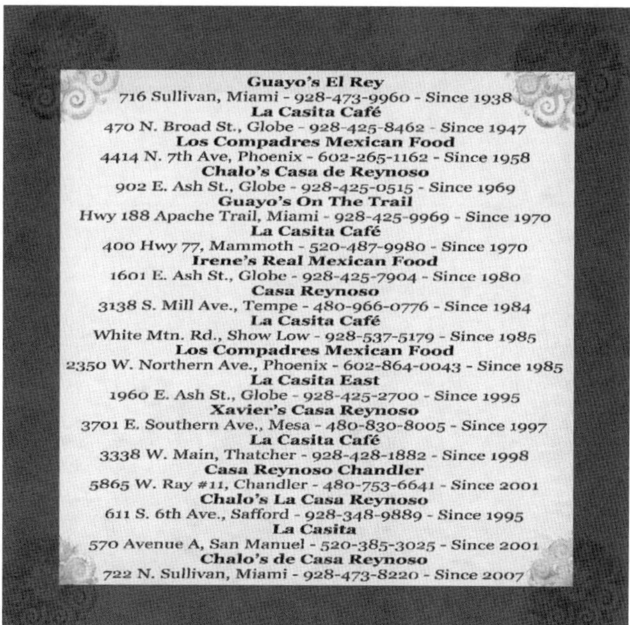

The poster lists all the Picazo/Reynoso restaurants and where to find them. *Author photo.*

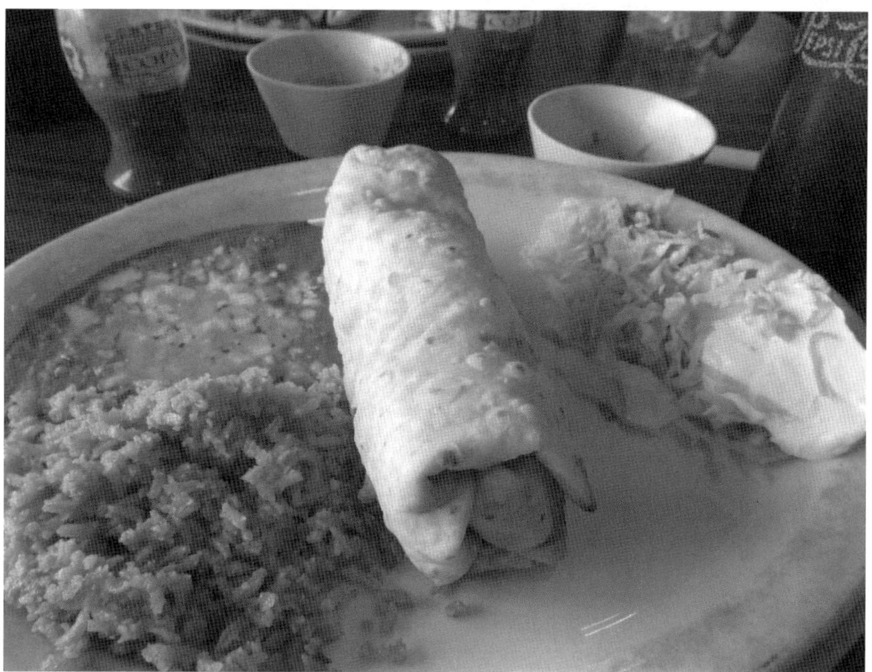

A chimi from Casa Reynoso in Globe. *Author photo.*

and grandchildren went on to open their own restaurants in Globe, Miami, Tempe, Mesa, Mammoth, San Manuel, Chandler, Thatcher, Show Low, Safford and Phoenix with names like La Casita, Chalo's Casa de Reynoso and Irene's Real Mexican Food.

Needless to say, Josefina and her sisters influenced or, better yet, created a certain style of Mexican food: Globe-Miami style. Juanita noted that even though everyone has chimis (and a full menu of other Mexican dishes), everyone adds their own touches, making the dishes different in subtle but delicious ways.

Here is a list of all the Reynoso/Picazo/Esparza family restaurants:

- Chalo's Casa Reynoso, Globe
- Guayo's El Rey, Miami
- La Casita Café, Globe
- La Casita East, Globe
- Guayo's on the Trail, Miami
- Los Compadres (2), Phoenix
- La Casita Café, Mammoth
- Casa Reynoso, Tempe
- Xavier's Casa Reynoso, Mesa
- Irene's Mexican Food, Globe
- La Casita Café, Show Low

NOT YOUR NANA'S CHIMICHANGAS

These unusual chimis prove that just about anything goes when it comes to creating a chimichanga.

Mi Patio, Phoenix

Mi Patio sits squarely on the corner of Seventh Avenue and Osborn Road in downtown Phoenix, just as it has ever since it first opened its doors in 1984.

Taking inspiration from the mistress of Hernando Cortés, who was known for decorating lush patios throughout Mexico, Rita Perez turned an abandoned gas station into a lovely little restaurant, creating a patio-like vibe. She opened to rave reviews for her simple food. Over the years, Mi Patio became a neighborhood favorite.

Today, the place is owned by Johnny Throuvalas and George and Stefano Daniolos, two brothers with Greek roots like Throuvalas, who purchased the place in 1988; George joined sometime in 2008, while Stefano has been around since 2013.

Johnny had owned a Greek restaurant in Chicago and fully intended to open another in Phoenix, but he soon realized that Mexican would be a better way to go: "I found out Mexican was number one," he said in a recent phone interview. "It was self-service and I changed that." Throuvalas noted that the long lines out the door discouraged customers. He made other changes but kept many of Perez's artistic touches.

The restaurant is filled with Mexican knickknacks, strings of chile peppers, sombreros, pottery, flowers and parrots of all shapes and sizes. A bar dominates the entryway; it's here where Mi Patio's award-winning and inexpensive margaritas are made.

Some of the employees have been there for decades, as have many customers. Elio, the bartender, has been mixing Mi Patio's famous margaritas for more than thirty years; Jorge, the head chef, has worked there for twenty-five years. "I never fire anybody," Throuvalas joked.

Throuvalas brought the flavors of Greece with him and blended them with Mexican items, fusion food long before it became popular. He also brought another remnant from his days in Chicago: something he calls the "Balloon Café," whereby the servers make balloons for every child who eats there.

The chimi menu here contains bean and cheese chimis, red or green chili, machaca and chicken. But then there is a list of Mi Patio Especiales that are truly out of the ordinary. There's the Baja chicken chimi that is topped with the house Baja cream cheese sauce, a thick, rich sauce that takes the basic chimi up a notch or two. A regular customer noted, "They use all white meat. I'm not sure what they marinate the chicken with, but it's to die for." Then there's the Patio chimi, with a choice of beef or chicken, topped with fresh, green tomatillo sauce.

But the two chimis that are truly off the grid are the Gyros chimi and the Baja spinach and feta cheese chimi. The Gyros chimi is filled with tender strips of beef with tomatoes and onions cooked to near melting in a sauce redolent with Mediterranean spices. To finish off this unusual chimi, Mi Patio pours lots of cool, creamy tzatziki sauce on top. The Greek flavors show up again in the Baja spinach and feta cheese chimi. This chimi was named the "Best Chimichanga in Phoenix 2017" by *Phoenix New Times*. Not to rest on those laurels, another writer from the same paper called it the "Essential

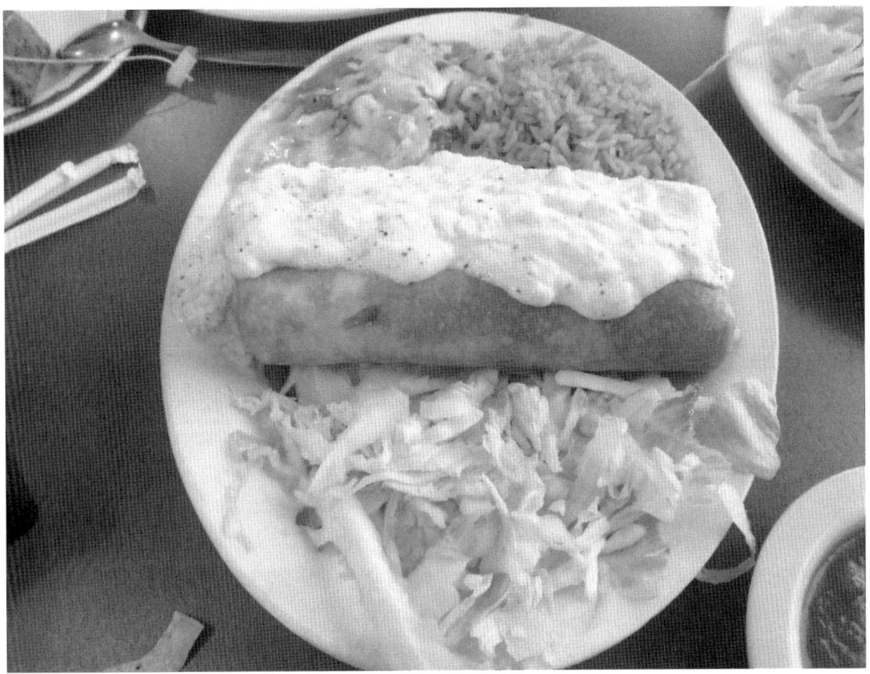

The Gyros chimi from Mi Patio in Phoenix. *Author photo.*

Mexican Restaurant Dish to Order with a To-Go Box." Oodles of spinach are blended with feta cheese and then packed into a flour tortilla that is then fried; for a final flourish it is baked with more of the Baja sauce until the topping melts. (This combo is also found in enchiladas and an appetizer dip.)

An appetizer of eight red and green chile mini-chimis is also on the menu.

Mi Patio continues to be a local favorite thanks to the many offerings on the menu and great service. "We keep everybody happy," Throuvalas said.

Chile Relleno Chimichanga: Agave Mexican Restaurant, Flagstaff

The majority of restaurants in this book have been around for decades—some are even considered historic—but Agave Mexican Restaurant in Flagstaff is so new the paint is barely dry on the bright colorful chairs. But since it opened its doors in 2014, Agave has made a name for itself with a full menu of traditional dishes and a few new creations.

Christian Valencia is the young owner and chef who earned his skills working in various restaurants for more than fifteen years. During that time, in the back of his mind, he knew that he wanted more out of life. So, after scrimping and saving, he was able to open his own place. He painted the walls in bright, sunny colors, hung Mexican knickknacks and art on the walls and pulled out a stack of family recipes.

The location along Route 66 is ideal, just outside Flagstaff. Dinner comes with a show if you are fortunate to get a table along the large picture window with up-close views of Route 66. But any seat in the house will do once the food arrives.

Here the chile relleno is a specialty, and in addition to any number of the regular fillings, Valencia prepares a chimichanga stuffed with one of his famous chile rellenos. A poblano chile is stuffed with a "mound" of cheese, wrapped in a flour tortilla and "lightly fried." The whole creation is then topped with Valencia's special chipotle sauce with guacamole and sour cream on the side.

Agave also has chicken, shredded beef and ground beef chimis that come with rice, beans, guacamole and sour cream, but a red sauce is served on the side, avoiding the conundrum of crispy chimi verses soggy chimi. Valencia hopes to grow his business with live music and other entertainment in the Cantina, where the bartenders mix up a wild assortment of margaritas. For the kids, Agave has real Mexican sodas.

Lobster and Goat Cheese Appetizer Chimi: Vincent at Camelback, Scottsdale

One might be surprised to find a chimichanga at a four-star classically French restaurant, but at Vincent on Camelback in upscale Scottsdale, the lobster chimichanga proves that chimis can be at home anywhere.

The lobster and goat cheese chimi is the creation of James Beard Award–winning chef Vincent Guerithault, who learned his craft in major kitchens in his native France. Vincent came to America in 1976 to work at Le Francais in Chicago and later moved to Phoenix, where he earned the attention of *New York Times* food editor Craig Claiborne and a host of other national foodies.

In Arizona, Vincent began to play with local ingredients—chiles, corn, beans and southwestern herbs and spices—incorporating them in to his classic French dishes. In 1986, he opened Vincent on Camelback in Scottsdale. Today, he oversees his self-named restaurant; a smaller, more intimate Market Bistro; a wildly popular weekly farmers' market; a corporate delivery service called Vincent's Van Go; and an extensive catering business.

Vincent on Camelback has been featured in *Gourmet* magazine, the *New York Times*, *Travel and Leisure* and countless culinary publications. The restaurant has won numerous national and international awards ranging from repeat wins as Best French Restaurant in the Valley by the *Phoenix New Times* and being named one of the top fifty restaurants in the world by *Restaurant* magazine.

In 1993, Vincent earned the James Beard America's Best Chef Southwest and in recent years was awarded the *Chevalier de L'Ordre de Merite Agricole* from the French government.

In spite of its posh setting, Vincent on Camelback is the ultimate family-run restaurant. Leevon, Vincent's wife, is essential to the success of the day-to-day workings. She oversees all those hidden things that go into making a restaurant a success. And their three sons, who grew up in the restaurant, cook at the farmers' market.

Vincent's chimi is a small wonder: a flour tortilla filled with poached lobster and creamy goat cheese, fried to perfection and served with a cilantro beurre blanc. The chimi isn't the only French take on Mexican fare; Vincent also makes a duck tamale and a smoked salmon quesadilla, as well as entrées and desserts touched with southwestern flavors.

Elegant and comfortable, uptown and cozy, chiles and beurre blanc—Vincent on Camelback brings a bit of France to the sunny Southwest.

Chimichanga Roll: Ryu Sushi, Gilbert

At Ryu Sushi, there's even more fusion food, like a flour tortilla wrapped around spicy tuna, spicy crab, cream cheese, avocado and jalapeños and then fried. Finishing touches include spicy mustard, eel sauce, scallions and sesame seeds.

Banana with Vanilla Ice Cream and Chocolate Sauce Chimi: Martanne's, Flagstaff

Martanne's Burrito Palace earned its popularity from making some of the best chilaquiles in the state. Chilaquiles is a simple dish of fried torn corn tortillas simmered in a chile sauce and is often eaten at breakfast with an egg. Shredded chicken or pork can also be added for a heartier meal. It can be served anytime at any meal. At Martanne's, it's one of the many popular breakfast items.

Located on Historic Route 66, Martanne's was originally owned by Gloria Martan, a woman from Nogales. In the early days, it was known as the Franciscan Café, but then Martan took over and changed the name and the menu. When she purchased the place, she inherited a cook, Miss Alice, known for her great food and sassy attitude.

In 2001, Martan sold the restaurant, complete with Alice, to Anne Martinez, who then changed the name as a play on her first and last names. The place was tiny and cramped, so when a house on Route 66 went up for sale, the Martinez family moved the entire operation to the current site. Bigger and brighter, Martanne's still has a waiting list on weekends. Inside, the walls are painted bright reds, blues, greens and purples. Art by Emma Gardner displays Day of the Dead figures and adds a certain quirkiness to the atmosphere.

Chimichangas are on the menu and can come filled with a choice of meat and cheese and served enchilada style (red or green), with a finish topping of guacamole and sour cream. Rice and beans are served on the side.

But the pièce de résistance is the Banana and Caramelo chimichanga on the dessert portion of the menu. The kitchen takes a banana and some caramel, wraps them in a flour tortilla and fries them just like any other chimichanga. The result is a delicious, ooey-gooey mess that is tempered with cold vanilla ice cream and hot chocolate sauce.

The Martinezes have another restaurant in Flagstaff, Casa Duarte, that has many of the same dishes found at Martanne's, but sadly, the dessert chimi is not on the menu.

Breakfast Chimichanga: Ocotillo Restaurant

The well-established team at Ocotillo Restaurant in Central City, Phoenix, made quite a splash when it opened its new concept in 2016. With its gorgeous use of light and space and multi-dining spaces, dining here is as much about the design (by architect John Labhan) as it is the food.

Calling the food "New American Seasonal Cuisine," chefs Walter Sterling and Sasha Levine created an "Ode to Arizona" according to *Phoenix New Times* food writer Patricia Escarcega. The wine list, curated by well-respected sommelier Dave Johnson, has wines from the world over.

Finding a chimi on the menu alongside spicy grilled duck, Spanish grilled octopus and smoked salmon might seem incongruous. The breakfast chimi is only found on the brunch menu and is filled with scrambled eggs, chicken, black beans and cheese and then bathed in a spicy green chili sauce, sprinkled with queso fresco and cilantro. The chimi won high praise from critics near and far.

Although Ocotillo is not in any way a Mexican restaurant, its breakfast chimichanga holds its own against any other chimis found in the Valley.

La Casita Special: La Casita, Bisbee

If you just can't make up your mind as to what type of chimi you want, La Casita can help. Its "special" chimi has shredded beef, shredded chicken, red chili, green chili, beans and rice all in one chimi.

Seafood Chimi or the Picadillo Chimi: Plaza Bonita, Cottonwood

The seafood chimi is listed with all the other seafood items offered at Plaza Bonita, while the picadillo is found in the combination section. The first combines shrimp, crab, scallops and veggies and finished off with a cream sauce. The picadillo is a secret family recipe.

Ultimate Chimi: Blue Agave Café, Phoenix

This is another chimi that combines multiple flavors and textures to satisfy whatever you might crave. Slow-roasted pork, rice, pinto beans, mixed cheese, green chili sauce and pico de gallo wrapped in a large tortilla shell and fried and then served with chipotle cream sauce, jalapeño cream sauce and chipotle puree. It also comes with sour cream and guacamole on the side.

Flagstaff

Arizona's northernmost city, Flagstaff, is fast becoming a foodie haven. At an elevation of seven thousand feet, Flagstaff is surrounded by the largest stand of Ponderosa pine in the world. Set among the San Francisco Peaks, the area is filled with raw beauty.

This lofty position allows for stunning views of both land and sky. The Lowell Observatory, home to intensive astronomical research, is located above the city, and visitors can experience the skies day and night at the observatory.

Winter is a true season in Flagstaff, and winter sports are plentiful, although sports enthusiasts can stay busy year-round thanks to mild weather in the other seasons.

Route 66 travels through the city, and Flagstaff has honored the "Mother Road" by maintaining many historical buildings and sites. The Burlington Northern Santa Fe Rail line also bisects the city. The two transportation routes make Flagstaff a crossroads of travel and trade. Northern Arizona University is also located here.

At the Javelina Cantina in Flagstaff, chimis can be ordered à la carte or as part of a combo plate with a choice of one or two other items (taco, enchilada, chile relleno, tostada, tamale or burrito). This is recommended only for the heartiest of eaters.

Ancient Native America tribes (Sinagua and Anazazi) lived in the area for centuries in cliff dwellings that are still visible, and today, the Hopi, Navajo, Kaibab-Paiute, Havasupai and Hualapai groups live on thirty-one thousand miles of tribal lands. The Native American culture is celebrated and honored as part of what makes Flagstaff such a vibrant city. The flavors and cooking styles of Native America are evident in restaurants in Flagstaff—even the chimichangas are different.

Indeed, the restaurants featured here have a full roster of regular chimis, but they also offer some intriguing takes.

El Tapatio

In the early 1990s, Francisco Espinoza and brothers Guillermo and Manny Gutierrez were working together at a Mexican restaurant in Grand Junction, Colorado. Espinoza decided that he wanted to break away and open his own Mexican restaurant featuring the foods of Jalisco, the Mexican state where he and the Gutierrez brothers had grown up.

So, in 1991, he opened a taco truck and called it El Tapatio. Within a year, he had opened a brick-and-mortar El Tapatio, and from there he opened three more in Colorado: one each in Parachute, Fruita and Delta—three communities within a twenty-five-mile stretch from one another.

Then a site caught his eye in Page, Arizona, a city just across the state line and ideally located on Lake Powell, a popular tourist spot. Things didn't go smoothly at first in Page, but then Espinoza called on his old friend Guillermo to take over. Thanks to Memo's restaurant experience and his handyman skills, the Page El Tapatio turned over a new leaf, which led to the restaurant in Flagstaff. This time, he brought Manny in all the way from Columbus, Ohio. The three are now co-owners.

Their home state, Jalisco, is located in west-central Mexico. Native American tribes lived there as long as fifteen thousand years ago. Spanish conquistadors reigned for decades. Guadalajara, Mexico's second-largest city, is located there. Part of the land is along the Pacific coast and includes the popular Puerta Vallerta. Mountains, lakes and plains provide a cornucopia of foodstuffs. Tequila originates in Jalisco, as do mariachis. All this makes Jalisco cooking vibrant and varied.

El Tapatio brings the best of Jalisco in one place. More than a half dozen unusual chimis are listed on the menu:

- Chimichangas de Mole: shredded chicken topped with a rich, sweet and savory sauce made with chiles, chocolate and peanut butter.
- Chimichangas de la Crema: shredded chicken topped with a cream sauce, which also has peanut butter as an ingredient (customers can ask to have the sauce made without peanut butter and El Tapatio is happy to oblige).
- Chipotle chimichangas: more shredded chicken, this time topped with a spicy sauce made with cream, peanut butter, chiles and chipotle chiles. It's fiery but also one of the most popular sauces on the menu.
- Fish chimichanga: tilapia, a fish found in Jalisco, is cooked with mushrooms, onions and tomatoes topped with the cream sauce.
- From the Sea: tilapia, baby shrimp, octopus, scallops, mushrooms, tomatoes and onions topped with cream sauce.
- Vegetarian: grilled vegetables with ranchero sauce on top and served with cholesterol-free ranch beans.
- Chili verde: pork in a green tomatillo sauce topped with green chili.
- Apple chimi for dessert: the apples are softened in a syrup before being rolled in a tortilla and fried. All this is smothered with chocolate and strawberry sauces and whipped cream. Sort of like a banana split.

For those who can't make up their minds, there is the Tapatio chimichanga plate with three chimis—one mole, one crema and one pork with the house green sauce. You can also order a chimi as part of a combination plate.

The chimis here are not as big as those found in most places, but they come two to an order. El Tapatio is a must if you're looking for a chimi that's just a little different.

Red Rock Country

Red Rock Country is, thanks to old western movies and television shows, the image that most people have of Arizona—at least if they've never visited. Towering mesas with shades of red and gold, huge expanses of land that seem to melt into the vast sky, rocky rivers, lush forests, ghost towns and all manner of cowboy life can be found there. But there are surprising modern touches as well.

The communities in the area range from chic Sedona, known for high-end shopping, dining and spas, to tiny Cottonwood, where traces of the mines that brought hundreds of people to the area in the 1800s stand like ghostly guards. There's Prescott, a happening mountain town rich with history, and Jerome, a mining town turned ghost town turned artist colony. Just a short drive from the Grand Canyon, the Verde Valley is a popular tourist destination year-round.

Mexican restaurants are plentiful, but unlike in other parts of the state, the food is influenced by the many Native American tribes that lived here decades before any Spanish conquistadors marched through. Chimichangas aren't as prevalent, but the ones that appear on menus are done up in tasty ways.

Sedona

El Rincon Restaurante Mexicano

Since even before it became a formal town, Sedona has been known as a center for spirituality and New Age mindfulness, but this Red Rock Country destination offers visitors so much more. Eclectic galleries and museums can be found around every corner. Shops are filled with one-of-a-kind items for just about any taste. For the nature lover, hikes, rock climbing and fishing are minutes away. History buffs will be in their glory. Culturally, Native Americans call this area home, and the influences are abundant.

Restaurants in town range from high-end dining to tiny cafés, Asian to Italian, burgers to barbecue—and, of course, Mexican. And it is here in Sedona, at El Rincon restaurant, where you'll find a most unusual chimichanga.

Demetri Wagner moved to Jerome, the mining town turned ghost town turned hippie haven, in 1973. He was a silversmith by trade and, by his own admission, "a California hippie complete with long hair and a Volkswagen van." He had a shop in Tlaquepaque, a lovely arts-and-crafts "village" in Sedona where visitors could watch artisans at work and purchase unique items. Sedona at that time was barely a dot on the map with only one stoplight.

He also befriended Ron Santillon, another artist, and soon was enjoying meals at Santillon's family home. Long a Mexican food fan, he raved about the food prepared at the Santillons', which was a blend of Mexican and Navajo dishes, a nod to Santillon's mother, who was Navajo, and his father, who was a Mexican from Spain. Wagner loved the food so much that when a small space opened in Tlaquepaque in 1976, he and Ron opened a restaurant, calling it El Rincon ("the Corner").

Tlaquepaque was an ideal spot for a Mexican restaurant with its adobe walls, shady ancient sycamores, tiled roofs, bubbling fountains, riots of colors from seasonal flowers and plants—all reminiscent of a peaceful Mexican village. El Rincon was situated in the heart of all this beauty, and dining on the patio with Oak Creek bubbling alongside was (and remains) a great respite from a busy day of sightseeing in Sedona.

Wagner had a $6,000 loan from his mom, Gloria Morrow, who had just relocated to the Verde Valley. "The day we opened, Sedona went wild," Wagner said. The restaurant took off like a shot, and in spite of the fact that after the first day there was only a small amount of change in the register, Wagner was able to pay back his mom in nineteen days.

Wagner and Santillon made an agreement that if and when they became successful, they would pay themselves $1,000 per month. Santillon and his family were in the kitchen, and Wagner took care of the front of the house. But he noted, "I learned all the ingredients and how to make the food."

The chimis were especially popular. People had never seen anything like them. All the food at El Rincon was rooted in Native American flavors and textures. Today, the website boasts that they are "the originators of 'Arizona

Style' Mexican food, a blend of traditional Mexican food with local Navajo/ Hopi Indian influences."

Instead of using flour tortillas, the chimis are made with a dough made from flour, water and baking powder. Depending on where you live, the mix is called Navajo fry bread or *sopapillas* (Mexican). The dough is rolled out in an oval of sorts, filled with chicken, beef, beans and even shrimp and then folded over. The ends are crimped like a pie, and then the whole thing is deep-fried. Topped with cheese and enchilada sauce, the chimis are finished off in the oven. The result is crispy edges, like a pie, with the rest of the chimi being soft and dumpling-like. "It's like a grande emapanada," said Wagner's son, Jeramya, who is now an integral part of the whole operation. Today, the chimis are made exactly as they were in the early days.

As successful as the restaurant was, not everything ran as planned. One night about three months into the operation, as Wagner was closing the restaurant for the day, Santillon showed up and told Wagner that he'd finish up and asked for the register drawer with all the day's money. Wagner handed it over but later realized that something was amiss and felt that he was being shoved out of the business. So, at about four o'clock in the morning, he went back to the restaurant with his van, gathered all the pots and pans and the register and went home.

When the workers, mostly from Santillon's family, showed up the next day, they realized what happened. They patched together a few utensils and tried to make the restaurant work. That lasted about a week and was an utter failure. They had the recipes, but all the other elements, like ordering food and balancing the books, were not part of their skill sets.

So, Santillon went to Wagner and, in spite of the fact that he had never invested any cash, asked to be bought out. Sticking with the $1,000-per-month agreement, Wagner paid his soon-to-be-ex-partner $3,000, $1,000 for each month in business, and Wagner set to reopen the restaurant alone. "We opened a week later," said Wagner.

Wagner called on his mom, Gloria, and sisters, Candace and Cindy. Gloria was a great cook with midwestern roots, and in spite of the fact that she had no idea how to make an enchilada sauce, she took over the kitchen. Wagner's brother, Rob, helped as well, plating food with absolutely no experience in a professional kitchen.

The first order came in, a chicken burro, and no one in the kitchen could figure out how to roll the burro so it held everything together. By the time they had it plated, every table in the restaurant was filled. "I have no idea how we got through those first days," Wagner said. But today, El Rincon remains one of the best restaurants in Sedona.

No other Mexican restaurant prepares chimis the way El Rincon does. The chimis are one of if not the most popular items at the restaurant. Served enchilada style, with either red or green chili sauce, cheese and onions, a chimi at El Rincon is a must-order item. Jeramya also noted that in spite of the unusual presentation, most of the comments are more about the flavor and quality ingredients. Because the kitchen is so small, just about everything is made to order with quality, fresh ingredients. Chili and sauces are made daily.

Wagner credited much of the success to his employees, many of whom have been at the restaurant for decades. Chaly and Luis in the kitchen have worked there for twenty years. "They do a phenomenal job," said Wagner. The bartender has been making El Rincon's famous margaritas for thirty-eight years. "Nothing has changed," said Wagner, referring to the food and service. But that doesn't mean eating at El Rincon is old hat—just consistent and reliable.

Gloria died in 2012, and these days, son Jeramya handles the kitchen with the knowledge, respect and passion that his father and grandmother instilled in him. He has visions for the future, perhaps adding another level of cooking with ancient grains and ingredients used by the Native Americans.

Chimis also appear as desserts. They are filled with apple, cherry, peach and sometimes chocolate. And the fry bread is also used in another unusual dish, the Navajo pizza, where a large round of dough is fried and then topped with meats, cheese, chile, salsa and all manner of flavorful items. "No one else in America makes food like we do," said Wagner.

A visit to El Rincon and eating one of its amazing chimis is a must for any trip to Sedona.

Along the Salsa Trail, several local specialties found nowhere else in Arizona but do appear on just about every participating restaurant's menus are chalacas and Big Daddy. Chalacas are basically a bowl created from corn masa that is deep-fried and then filled with an assortment of beans, beef or chicken, lettuce and tomatoes. The Big Daddy is a large deep-fried flour tortilla topped with refried beans, melted cheese, lettuce, tomato and sometimes red or green chile. The green chili tends to outsell the red, according to Diane Hoopes of Casa Manana. The Little Daddy, a smaller version, is available for those with smaller appetites.

Eastern Arizona

The Salsa Trail

Graham County is an area rich with history, natural beauty, huge family farms and ranches and some fantastic Mexican food. Sonoran dishes are influenced by neighboring New Mexico food, redolent with chiles that add heat and smoke.

The Reynoso family of the Globe-Miami area got their start in the restaurant business with two restaurants in Thatcher and Safford, but both sites are now closed.

In 2005, as a way to promote Graham County and all the great food found in the area, a group of locals created the Salsa Trail. With Safford as the starting point, the Salsa Trail meanders through Graham County (and parts of Greenlee and Cochise Counties), traversing some of the prettiest countryside Arizona has to offer. Today, about a dozen family-run restaurants in the area belong to the group. Traveling along the trail takes more than a day, especially if you decide to take advantage of the myriad activities such as hiking, museums, historical sites, wineries, an international observatory, orchards and more. But if you time everything just right, you can eat at nearly all of the restaurants in the group.

Not all of the Salsa Trail restaurants have chimis on their menus, but rest assured, the chimis that are served on the Salsa Trail are tasty. This is a fine example of culinary tourism.

Casa Manana

Emma and Gabi Gabaldon opened Casa Manana in 1950 in the heart of downtown Safford. It was one of only two restaurants in town at the time. From humble beginnings, as a family home, Casa Manana has grown into a local tradition with half-hour waits on weekends.

The original owners were Gabi and Emma Gabaldon. Gabi took care of the front of the house, making sure that the mood was lively with jukebox music and his charming personality; Emma ran the kitchen with a confidence and plenty of family recipes.

Over the decades, the restaurant changed hands, each owner adding his or her own touches, but when current owner Diana Hoopes bought the place in 2004, she made a point of bringing back the landmark recipes that made Casa Manana a Safford favorite. People were thrilled. Today, chimis can be filled with Emma's original red chili, green chili, shredded chicken, a fiery machaca, refried beans or any of the other protein options found on the menu.

At Casa Manana, enchilada style means either a traditional red sauce or a creamy green enchilada sauce that Hoopes notes tastes great with the chicken chimis.

Being a part of the Salsa Trail means having great salsas, and the secret tomatillo sauce is a favorite here. And when they say "secret," they mean it! But fortunately, people can buy the packages of the spice mix that comes with instructions on how to make this award-winning salsa at home. You can purchase the mix at http://store.thecasamanana.com.

La Paloma

The tiny town of Solomon is about five minutes from Safford and two hours from Tucson and is the home to one of the most popular restaurants on the Salsa Trail.

La Paloma has been serving Sonoran dishes with a hint of New Mexico since the early 1950s, when it was known as Shorty's Bar. Back then, people would wait hours for a table because the food was so fine. There have been numerous owners over time, but it was someone called Pat Hernandez who changed the name to La Paloma. With infinite wisdom and a little help from the same cooks who worked at Shorty's, he kept the same recipes that people loved.

In 1986, Charles and Nancy Curtis purchased La Paloma. They made physical changes to the place and expanded into an adjoining building. But they, too, kept Shorty's recipes, daily grinding the fresh chiles used in the enchilada sauce and other dishes.

In 2008, the Curtises sold the place to Tom and Shelly Claridge, who in time sold the restaurant to the current owner, Nick Tellez. Tellez was an employee at La Paloma when he was in high school, working every position from dishwasher to manager. Tellez knew and loved La Paloma like it was his own, and so after college and a few years in restaurants in Phoenix, he returned to the area and purchased the site. Tellez made a point of retaining the dishes La Paloma was known for while adding a few touches of his own. The crowds still come in droves.

While the menu here has the usual list of chimis, the house specialty version is the chimichanga pollo verde. Chicken, green chiles, tomatoes and onions inside and a smothering of the house green chile chicken enchilada sauce, cheese, green onions and sour cream make this chimi one of a kind.

Salsa Trail Restaurants

- Casa Manana, Safford
- El Charro, Safford (not part of the Tucson group)
- El Coronado, Safford
- GiMee's, York
- Isabel's South of the Border, Willcox
- La Paloma, Solomon
- La Unica Tortilliaria and Taqueria, Willcox
- Manor House & Rock n' Horse Saloon, Safford
- Mechy's Mexican Food, Safford
- Michelle's Bar & Grill, Morenci
- Taco Taste, Safford
- Taylor Freeze, Pima

Chimis Along the Border

Douglas

Rumor has it that Arizona senator Dennis DiConcini loved the chimichangas from now closed La Fiesta in Douglas so much that he would pack hundreds of them in a thermal carrier to enjoy back in Phoenix.

Casa Segovia

Sadly, La Fiesta closed in 1988 (with a brief restart from 2008 to 2012 when the original owner, Martha Segovia, reopened the place), leaving Senator DiConcini in a quandary. But then, in 2016, something remarkable happened that cheered Douglas locals and, one would hope, Senator DiConcini.

The owners of the historic Gadsden Hotel were looking for help in reviving the lagging business. The restaurant was in shambles, and the solution was to ask Martha Segovia if she could possibly come in and run the restaurant for a year. Segovia was up for it but knew that she would need a helping hand, so she asked her granddaughter, Roxanne Samaniego, if she would be interested.

"I said yes!" said Samaniego.

After several months of hard work bringing the room and kitchen back to a workable and pleasant place to dine, Segovia and family christened the new place Casa Segovia in honor of Martha's husband and opened the doors in 2016. "Within three months, the place boomed. She had a pretty large following," said Samaniego. So much so that when the hotel was sold, the new owners, the Lopez family, insisted that Segovia stay.

These days, thanks to the extensive remodeling and the popularity of Casa Segovia, the hotel is experiencing a new life. At eighty-six, Martha still comes to work every day. "She oversees the kitchen now," her granddaughter said. The restaurant serves breakfast, lunch and dinner for hotel guests and locals alike. And those famous chimis that were a political favorite are still on the menu.

Bisbee

In its heyday, Bisbee was home to nearly twenty thousand people, making it the largest city between St. Louis and San Francisco. Residents were miners and millionaires, shopkeepers and schoolmarms, ladies of the evening and lost souls.

In the 1900s, the mines in the Mule Mountains that surround Bisbee produced gold, copper, silver, lead and zinc. People came to Bisbee to get rich or make a new life. And while the miners spent their hard-earned cash at the many saloons that lined Brewery Gulch, other high-class citizens enjoyed the opera and a first-class library, watched baseball and played golf.

The mining boom continued into the twentieth century, but then in the mid-1970s, the mines dried up and people moved on. Bisbee became a virtual ghost town until the counterculture crowd discovered the place. Hippies moved into the abandoned homes, opened businesses in the once-thriving downtown area of Old Bisbee and saved Bisbee from oblivion.

Other, more establishment types followed, and today Bisbee is a happening home to a mixed bag of people who love their town. Quirky shops, art galleries, historic tours, restaurants and a laid-back lifestyle bring thousands of tourists to Bisbee for a day, a week and longer.

Santiago's

In the heart Old Bisbee, as the old center of town is called, sits the historic Medigovich Building. In previous times, the building housed a pharmacy, a bathhouse, a hotel, an ice cream parlor and a Western Union station. Today, it is the home to Santiago's, one of Arizona's "Best Restaurants" according to *Arizona Highways* magazine.

Owned by the Page family, who can trace their roots to turn-of-the-twentieth-century Arizona, the restaurant has an interesting connection to their great-grandfather Ferdinand Vingnbaux, who lived in Bisbee in the late 1890s. He owned the building for a time when he was the pharmacist. "We didn't find out about grandfather's pharmacy until we bought it," said Rob Page, chef and co-owner with the rest of his family. "We did a title search. We felt it was meant to be."

Originally from Douglas, where their grandfather moved, the Pages decided to make a move back to Bisbee when they saw that the town was undergoing a positive revival. The town council had passed an ordinance prohibiting large chain restaurants and other businesses from opening and operating in Bisbee. They loved Bisbee and wanted to help keep the town's low-key hip vibe.

They opened the town's first modern coffeehouse, Bisbee Coffee, in 1995 and now own and operate Bisbee Coffee, Bisbee Table and Santiago's. They also run Hotel San Ramon, which is located on the floor above Santiago's. "It's a family endeavor. My brother [Michael] is the marketing director. My wife [Suzanne] is a human resource professional. Mom [Georgia] runs the people side of things," said Page. Father Ed, a retired air force colonel, contributes his skills and wisdom and a lot of hard work. Sisters, children, cousins and a full assortment of relatives play vital roles in all the various restaurants' operations.

Their signature dish, *chilorio*, which shows up in not just the chimi but other items as well, is a recipe they got from one of the chefs. "We have a chef competition every month," Page said. "The winner gets $250 and a portion of the profits from their dish." Page explained that *chilorio* is from Oaxaca in central Mexico, where a lot of pork is raised. "It's marinated in red chiles, brown sugar and orange juice, there's a lot of citrus."

Ingredients for their restaurants are sourced as locally as possible: chiles and eggs come from nearby farms; tortillas are handmade in Naco, the Mexican border town just down the road from Bisbee; beans, tomatoes and onions are brought in from Kansas Settlement; and the pork comes from Chiricahua Pasture Raised Meats in Willcox, a farm community that is also home to several Arizona wineries.

Other chimis on the menu include shredded chicken or beef. Those in the know order guacamole that is made tableside and a margarita made from one of the dozens of tequilas Santiago's has curated.

In 2017, the Pages entered their salsa and tacos in the Southern Arizona Arts and Cultural Alliance annual Salsa, Tequila and Taco Challenge and won the whole thing. Page said they're looking forward to competing again; no word if the tacos will be made with *chilorio*.

Tumacácori/Tubac

Tumacácori's history began with a Pima Indian settlement long before Padre Eusebio Kino, a Jesuit priest, arrived. The padre established one of his many missions in 1691. But in 1751, a Pima Indian uprising—an oddity, given that the Pimas were known to be more peaceful than the neighboring Apaches—caused fear and uncertainty.

The mission was relocated, and as protection against any further attacks, a presidio (fort) was established in Tubac. Political and religious shenanigans in Spain resulted in the Jesuits being ousted, and Franciscans took over the mission.

Eventually, the Tubac garrison was moved to Tucson. The area was still part of Mexico, and in 1828, a decree from the Mexican government forced all Spanish residents to flee. In spite of the fact that a newer, larger church had been built by Fray Narcisso Gutierrez, the mission eventually was nearly abandoned by 1848.

Today, the area is a popular tourist spot. The mission and church remain in Tumacácori, and Tubac has grown into a world-renowned artists' colony with numerous shops and galleries. The annual Tubac Festival of the Arts attracts visitors by the thousands.

Wisdom's

Wisdom's Café could easily be missed as you travel south out of Tubac on the frontage road, also known as Old Nogales Highway, except for two things. Two giant metal chickens mark the entrance to the tiny adobe block building. You can't help but see them, and even if your destination wasn't this charming spot, curiosity might make you pull over.

First opened in 1927, by Howard and Petra Wisdom, the out-of-the-way spot attracts hundreds of diners annually. Most are tourists visiting artsy Tubac less than two miles north or the Tumacácori National Monument about two minutes south. But many are people who drive down from Tucson

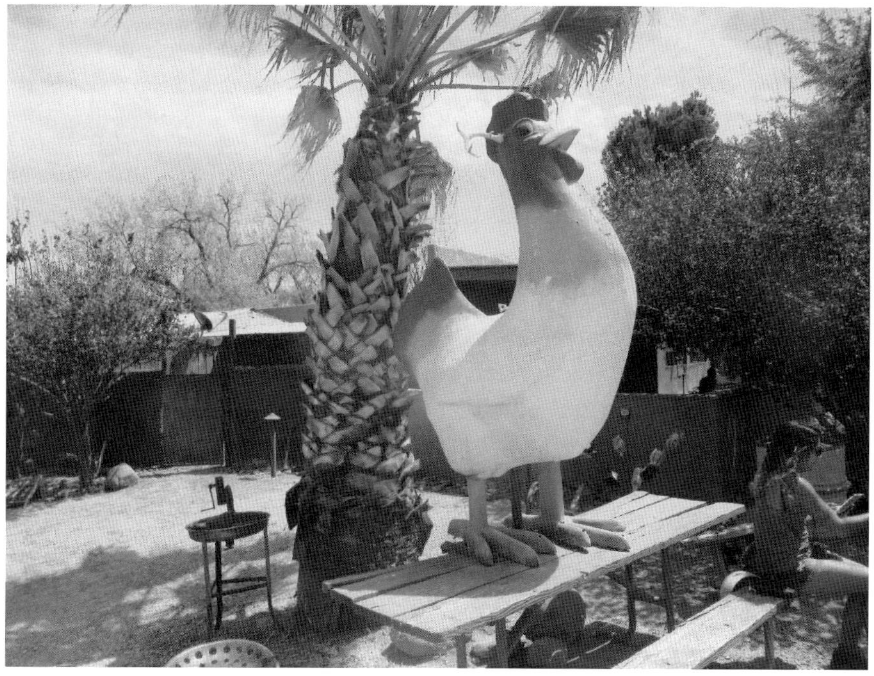

This giant chicken lets you know you've arrived at Wisdom's Café in Tumacacori. *Author photo.*

and Green Valley or up from Nogales just to have one of Wisdom's World-Famous Fruit Chimichangas.

Howard and Petra inherited the property from Petra's father and at first served only breakfast and adult beverages. Howard was a *real* cowboy and added an area where he held pop-up rodeos as entertainment. And since the café was located along the only route between Tucson and Nogales, Wisdom's Café was extremely popular. Then in 1979 came progress in the name of Interstate 19, and Wisdom's closed along with dozens of other tiny businesses on Nogales Highway.

But the Wisdoms weren't down yet. The following year, their son, Herb, and his wife, Irene, packed up everything they had and relocated to Tumacácori from California to help revive the business. Sisters Jennie Belle and Linda and brother Jesse pitched in, as did Irene's mom, who helped in the kitchen with two other women, Frances and Barbara; Barbara still works there. Their recipes are still used today.

Some of her recipes are the fillings used in Wisdom's chimichangas. Both shredded and ground beef are available as well as bean, but the chimi that

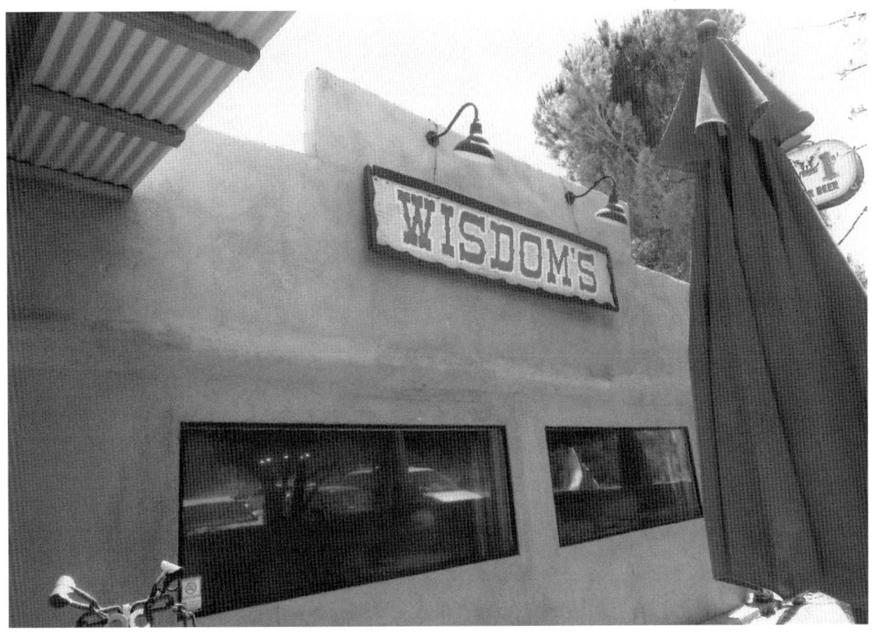

Exterior at Wisdom's. *Author photo.*

stands out here is the turkey. Plenty of savory moist turkey is packed into a flour tortilla and then fried to such a perfect crispiness that even if you decide to go enchilada style (red or green tomatillo), the outside literally crackles when you cut into one. The enchilada sauce holds a creamy texture and a mellow orange tone unlike others found elsewhere. "Our enchilada sauce tastes different and is such a lighter color because we use a chile paste from the Santa Cruz and Spice Company right down the street from us," said Celeste, "and have done so for decades."

The turkey is cooked low and slow overnight, and then in the morning, the turkey is shredded. The chimi at first doesn't seem to be as big as you might find elsewhere, but as you savor the tastes and textures (the red enchilada sauce is superb), you'll find that you may even have leftovers.

Herb had visions of following in his father's footsteps as a cowboy, but his talents as a softball player led to playing professionally with Eddie Feignor, "The King" of professional softball. Herb's love for the game continued for decades, and he established the Si Senor, senior men's league, where he and his teams won numerous championships. He sponsored countless youth softball teams and most recently built—much of it with his own money—a softball field for the children of the area.

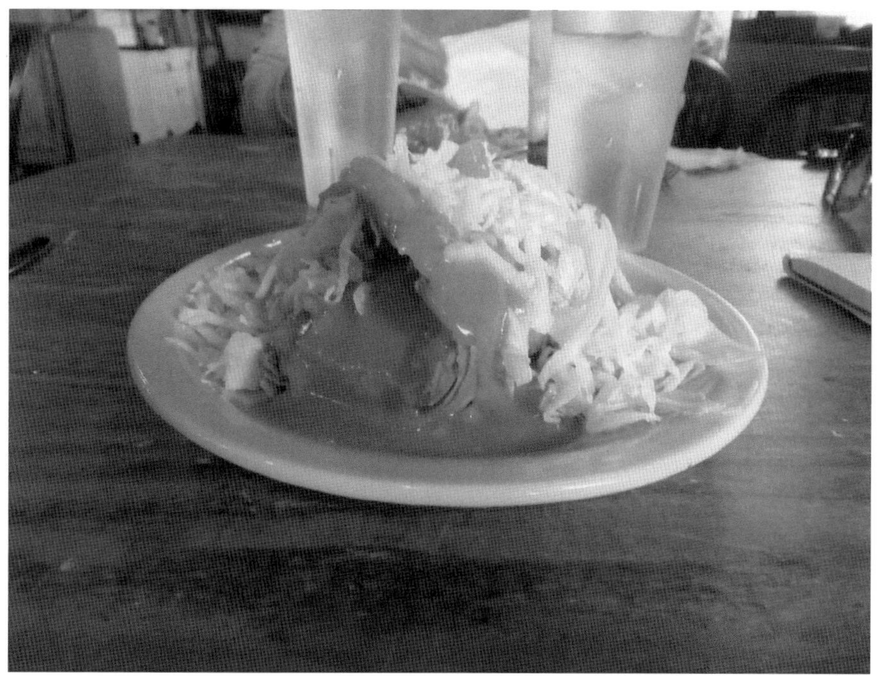

Wisdom's turkey chimi is one of a kind. *Author photo.*

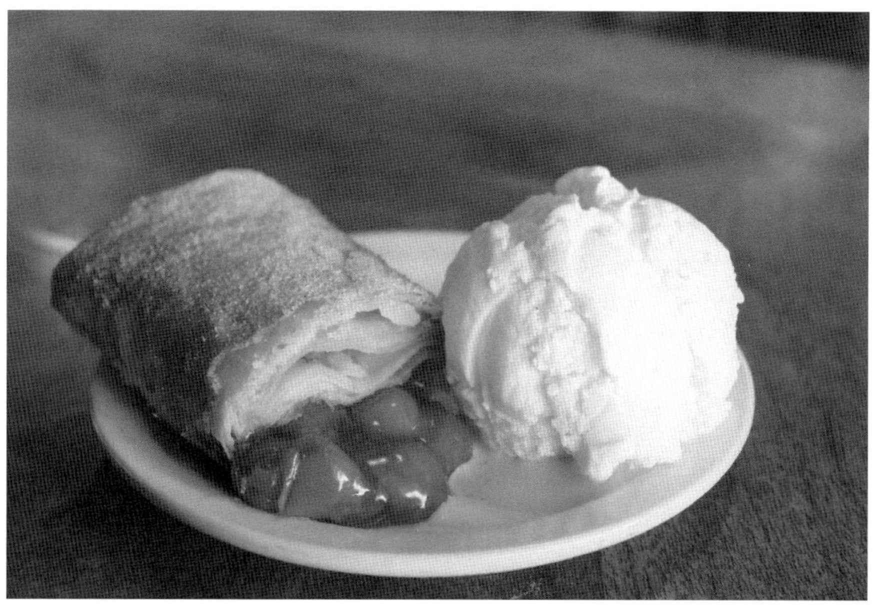

A cherry chimi unlike any other. *Courtesy of Wisdom's Café.*

Herb and Irene have passed the torch to their son, Cliff, and his wife, Celeste, who continue the family traditions. The walls at Wisdom's are filled with murals created by friends and family, colorful paintings, antiques, farm and cowboy gear, beer steins, dolls, a full assortment of both Herb and Cliff's softball career items and other whatnots often donated by customers.

Wisdom's World-Famous Fruit Chimi is the first item listed on the menu. The only dessert, other than the homemade ice cream, the beginnings of this treat sound vaguely familiar. A cook accidently dropped a jelly-filled tortilla in hot oil and voila!—a Wisdom tradition was born.

Unlike other dessert chimis, which are miniature versions, here they are full-size and take up the entire plate. Hot out of the fryer (it's recommended you order them when you order your entrée), these chimis are then rolled in cinnamon sugar and served with a scoop of Wisdom's vanilla ice cream. They put pies to shame, and there really isn't anything like them anywhere else in the state. Flavors include apple, cherry, peach, coconut crème, blueberry and a flavor of the month. Wisdom's Café is also known for outstanding tamales and big, potent margaritas.

The Wisdoms opened a smaller eatery just up the road in Tubac called Wisdom's Dos. The place has counter service, and the menu is slightly different, with the only chimi on the menu being those World-Famous Fruit Chimichangas.

BENSON

Benson was founded as a railroad junction and played an important part in the growth of the nearby mining industry. A mere forty-five miles southeast of Tucson, today Benson is where people stop on the way to and from Kartchner Caverns State Park. The caves were only discovered in 1974 and remained a secret for ten more years; the site formally opened as a park in 1999. Kartchner Caverns is one of the state's most popular attractions. The San Pedro River, which runs through Benson, attracts birders from around the world.

Mi Casa

Mi Casa is the kind of place that one could drive past and not really notice: the tiny building, the dirt parking lot, the simple sign. But people have noticed, with some driving from as far away as Phoenix just to eat at this "hidden gem" in Benson. With only twenty-four seats, there is often a wait, but fans don't seem to mind.

Owned and operated by Andy and Santa Sutton, Mi Casa's food isn't strictly Sonoran because Santa, who does all the cooking, is from La Paz, Mexico, which is the capital of Baja California Sur. The recipes she uses are generations old.

La Paz dishes mean plenty of seafood, and shrimp plays an important role on the Mi Casa menu. Santa and Andy met in La Paz while he was in the service. They operated a food truck for several years before opening the free-standing restaurant.

And while the influences at Mi Casa are from Central Baja, Sonoran dishes are on the menu. There are only two chimichangas listed—the Baja and the California—but the choice of fillings is numerous: ground beef, charbroiled chicken or beef, roasted pork green chili or, as a salute to La Paz, grilled shrimp. The Baja also has beans and pico de gallo and is topped with a choice of secret red or green sauce (or both), cotija cheese and cilantro. The California, which comes without beans or pico de gallo, is topped with the special "Casa Sauce," cilantro and both cheddar and cotija cheeses.

Mi Casa is only open during the week in order to give the Suttons family time.

TOMBSTONE

Tombstone boasts being the "Town Too Tough to Die." Stories abound about Wyatt Earp, Doc Holliday, the Clanton brothers, Big Nose Kate and the most famous showdown of all, the Gunfight at the OK Corral. Founded by Ed Schieffelin in 1877, Tombstone grew around Ed's strike and silver mine.

The call of silver attracted anyone looking to make it rich or just start a new life, and the population of Tombstone grew to about five thousand people by 1881. As in most western towns of the time, the citizens were a mixed bag of miners, cowboys, ladies of the evening (of which there were quite a few), Native Americans, Mexicans, Chinese and wandering souls.

Two fires, one in 1881 and another the following year, nearly reduced the town to ashes. But like the phoenix of myth, Tombstone rebuilt itself thanks to the pluck and tenacity of the citizenry.

Tombstone was the fastest-growing city between St. Louis and San Francisco. Businesses sprang up to meet the needs and wants of Tombstone residents. Saloons were plentiful—after all, a man needed someplace to quench his thirst and relax after a long, lonely time prospecting. There were plenty of bordellos as well, but entertainment also included the Schiefflin Hall, built by Ed's brother, for respectable folks.

Around 1879, the peripatetic Wyatt Earp and his brothers arrived in Tombstone. The Earps almost immediately became embroiled in a battle with "The Cowboys," a group of no-good-niks who were known to terrorize the townsfolk. The feud continued for years, with the famous shootout at the OK Corral being only one part of the fiery relationship between the two groups. In that famous shootout (which lasted a total of twenty-four seconds), Cowboys, Billy Clanton and Tom and Frank McLaury were killed. In revenge, the Cowboys killed Morgan Earp and maimed Virgil in an assassination attempt. Wyatt, his other brother Warren and Doc Holliday pursued the rest of the gang as payback.

Today, Tombstone is a "living town," with about 1,300 year-round residents who happily celebrate the history of their town by welcoming thousands of visitors from around the world. Boot Hill, where many of the aforementioned players are buried; the Birdcage Saloon; Big Nose Kate's Saloon; underground mine tours; and daily reenactments of the shootout are popular attractions.

The attempt on Virgil Earp's life came from a shot that was fired from a second-floor window of the Owl Café and Hotel, now called the Longhorn Restaurant. The building went through various incarnations, everything from the Bucket of Blood Saloon to the Holiday Water Company.

The Longhorn, Tombstone's oldest continuously operating restaurant, serves only one chimi, but some say it's the best in town. Here's the description straight off the menu: "*Ein treditioneller mexikanischen Lederbissen wir nehmen unser langsan gegartes….*" As a nod to all the international visitors, the menus are in German, Spanish and English. Here's the English copy: "A classic Mexican treat. We take our slow cooked shredded beef, tomatoes, mild green chiles and spices, then roll 'em in a large flour tortilla and deep fry it to a golden brown. Garnished with lettuce, cheese and tomatoes. Served with refried beans and rice…Have it Enchilada Style…Add Guacamole."

Please note that chimichanga in German is still "chimichanga."

ARIZONA'S WEST COAST

The Colorado River enters Arizona at the Utah-Arizona state line. From there, it travels southwest, reaching the California-Arizona line, crosses into Mexico and empties into the Gulf of California.

Humans saw the potential of a strong source of water and built dams and reservoirs along the way. The most ambitious was Hoover Dam. Built between 1931 and 1936, the dam forever changed the landscape and life along the Colorado. Formerly called Boulder Dam, the purpose was multifold: improve irrigation, control flooding and provide electricity. The construction offered thousands much-needed jobs, but more than one hundred people died during the construction.

Lake Powell, Lake Mead, Lake Mohave and Lake Havasu were also created, and communities sprang up near the reservoirs, eventually growing into towns and cities. Page is the northernmost Arizona city on the river. Bullhead City, Lake Havasu City, Parker and Yuma lie along the river.

Today, visitors and locals enjoy the myriad recreational activities the lakes and river offer. The original London Bridge is a major tourist attraction at Lake Havasu. Bullhead City sits across the border from Laughlin, Nevada, and provides respite from the lights and noise of its sister city. Parker stretches along sixteen miles of the river and is a playground for water sports. And Yuma, a city that played a major role in Arizona's history since the late 1800s, has grown into a destination spot thanks to the river and proximity to Mexico.

Chimis here may appear smaller because *sobaqueros* are not as readily available, but the cooks spare no lack of creativity when it comes to chimis on the coast.

Bullhead City: El Palacio & Casa Serrano, Parker

Angilberto Serrano met his wife, Isabel, while working together at a restaurant. She helped him learn English, and they fell in love. Working his way up from dishwasher to chef, they moved from California and in 1981 opened El Palacio in Bullhead City.

Today, the family owns four restaurants located throughout northern Arizona and into Nevada under two names, Casa Serrano and El Palacio. Casa Serrano restaurants can be found in Mohave Valley, Lake Havasu and Laughlin, Nevada. El Palacio are home in Bullhead City and Kingman. The

Kingman site was sold by the Serranos to one of their workers, Gilbert Correro.

Like his former boss, Correro had been a dishwasher who worked his way up the kitchen ladder and purchased the business sometime around 2012. That site is located in a historic former ice plant on Route 66.

The Kingman El Palacio was named one of Arizona Highways' "Best Restaurants" in 2014. There was a small controversy a while back when the building was painted a bright greenish yellow. Some Kingman residents objected that the colors didn't fit in with other historic buildings. But the hubbub settled down quickly when people realized that a successful business was more important.

The Serranos take pride in making everything from scratch on a daily basis. Angilberto insists on only the best and freshest ingredients. At a young sixty-three, he's still in the kitchen every day. "He doesn't slow down," said Anthony. And neither does Isabel, who oversees the office and paperwork for the 120 employees.

Son Anthony was two when his parents opened their first restaurant, and he's been in the kitchen ever since. After earning his degree in culinary management at Le Cordon Bleu College of Culinary Arts, he returned to continue the family tradition. His recipes have won numerous awards throughout the state, and in 2016, he was a Recipe Champion at the World Food Championship, a multifaceted event that pits chefs from all over the United States against one another in what has been called the "Ultimate Food Fight." He competed on the Food Network's *Chopped* in January 2018, and the restaurant's giant burro, El Bandito, was featured on the channel's *Ginormous Food.*

At all the restaurants, in addition to regular chimis, two special chimis are served: a seafood chimi and a steak carbon style. The seafood chimi, created by Angilberto, is filled with shrimp, imitation crab and pico de gallo. The steak chimi contains steak marinated in soy sauce and then grilled (carbon).

TEN OTHER CHIMICHANGA FINDS

Two Amigos: Oysters, Kingman
Oysters is included not so much because the chimi is so special but because one menu choice has both a chicken chimichanga smothered in sour cream and cheese *and* a ground beef burrito served enchilada style. Only for the big eaters. Rest assured that a single chimi is also available.

The 1946 Chimichanga: Cretin's, Yuma
An extra-large chimi filled with chicken or machaca and served enchilada style, named after the year the restaurant opened.

Original Blue Adobe Grill, Phoenix
Christmas chimichanga: any chimi topped with both red enchilada and green enchilada sauces.

El Rancho, Payson
Fajita chimichanga: available with shrimp, beef or chicken with onions, green peppers, green chiles and pico de gallo.

Rosa's, Tucson
Any chimi served Ortega style: a creamy "green" sauce that Rosa Ortega created in 1970 when she first opened her restaurant not far from the University of Arizona.

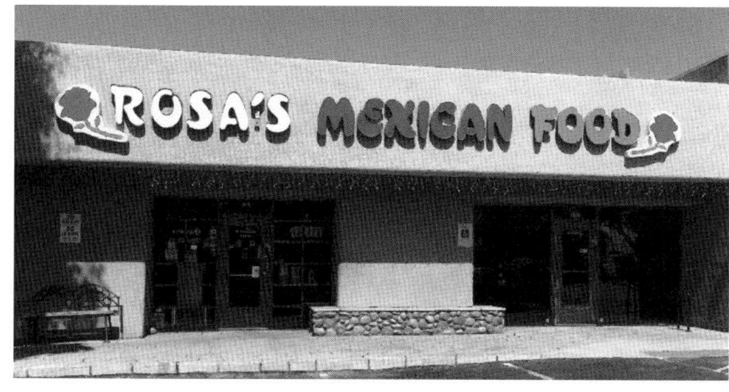

Rosa's has been serving great food for three generations. *Author photo.*

Mateo's Mexican Restaurant, Show Low
Only two chimis are available—carne asada or chicken—but the Baja sauce adds a special touch. The creamy sour cream sauce has horseradish in it, but the rest of the ingredients are an old family secret.

Mango's Mexican Café, Mesa
While the site does not have any specific specialty chimichanga, Mango's version has been called "one of the best dishes in greater Phoenix" by the local press and has even been named the "Best Chimi" in the past "Best of" features.

Rosita's Place, Phoenix
Although the site doesn't specify any particular chimi, the *Phoenix New Times* named Rosita's Place's chimi the "Best Chimichanga" in its 2016 annual "Best of" issue.

Chimichanga Blanco: Salsa Brava, Flagstaff
The smoked chicken here takes chicken chimis to a whole other level, and the house-made cilantro cheese sauce is a special touch.

Potato and Egg Chimichanga: La Indita, Tucson
Maria Garcia, a Tarasca Indian (La Indita means the "little Indian woman"), makes food influenced by her Native roots and time spent raising a family on the Tohono O'odham reservation. Her tacos, tamale and enchiladas egg chimi are great for breakfast, lunch or dinner.

IF YOU'RE EVER IN...

Honey, I'm in the mood for a chimichanga!
—Dustin Hoffman as Bernie Focker, Meet the Fockers

Granted, this book is about Arizona chimichangas, but the phenomenal popularity of chimis has resulted in chimis being found literally worldwide. Many of the creations are unusual, but one place authentic chimis can be found is in Charleston, West Virginia, at a little place called Mi Cocina de Amor. Owned and operated by Frank Gonzales III and his wife, Julia, the food served here is about as Tucson as it gets.

Mi Cocina de Amor

The inspiration for including chimichangas in Ken Lamberton's *Chasing Arizona: One Man's Yearlong Obsession with the Grand Canyon State* was a chimi he had as a child at Pancho's in Tucson. He described the chimi in such detail and with such reverence that you can almost taste the green chili and hear the crunchy fried tortilla.

Pancho's was a stalwart in Tucson for decades, and the mere mention of the name to longtime Tucsonans elicited responses of fond remembrance of good food and good times.

Frank "Pancho" Gonzales Sr. came from humble beginnings and worked from the time he was seven years old shining shoes. He washed school busses and caddied golf, where he made connections that would later prove to be important in the success of his business.

Chimichangas are the favorite food of Marvel Comics' Deadpool, mainly because he liked to say "chimichanga" over and over.

In 1946, when he and wife, Julietta, opened the first Pancho's in Tucson, it was practically the only authentic Mexican restaurant in midtown. The room was barely big enough for the half dozen tables he had built himself. But people didn't care. They came for the delectable food, especially the chimichangas. The business grew with a larger building and eventually two other restaurants.

His son, Frank Jr., managed the restaurants, although both Pancho and Julietta remained active in the business. Pancho died in 1969 and Frank Jr. in 2010, but by that time, the businesses had been sold.

The flavors that Lamberton so lovingly described seemed to have faded into the universe, in Tucson at least. But on the other side of the country, Pancho's live on. Today, Frank Gonzales III owns and operates Mi Cocina de Amor in, of all places, Charleston, West Virginia. He along with his wife, Julia, serve the same dishes that his grandparents served in Tucson, much to the delight of Charlestonians. Grandmother Julietta's special enchiladas are on the menu, as are an assortment of chimichangas (you can get chimichangitas as an *antojito*). And, of course, Ken Lamberton's

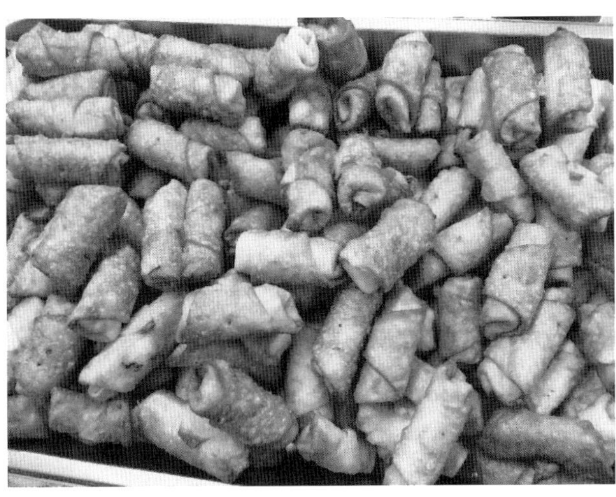

Mini-chimis from Mi Cocina de Amor. *Courtesy of Frank Gonzales III.*

memorable craving, the green chili chimi, is on the menu, made the same way as the day he ate one way back when.

So, if you happen to be in Charleston and get a hankering for an authentic chimichanga, head over to Mi Cocina di Amor. You won't be disappointed.

TRY THIS AT HOME

Considering people have been frying foods since the fifth millennium BC and that we live in an age where everything from candy bars to whole turkeys are deep-fried, the idea of a deep-fried burro is not so outlandish. Someone, somewhere must have said, "Hey, what if I throw this burro into a fryer?" Many people talk about having chimichangas at home as they were growing up, but it took the invention of a commercial deep-fat fryer to elevate the chimi to restaurant status.

Skip Jacob, of Tucson's Club 21, recalled a three- or four-gallon cooking pot filled with hot oil (often lard) with a wire basket. Cooks would place the food in the basket and lower it into the hot oil, and minutes later, they'd have a golden crispy whatever. He also spoke about frying both tacos and burros in cast-iron pans. The pan of hot oil wasn't deep enough for submerging the food, so it was cooked first on one side and then flipped over to finish the item. In deep-frying, the food is immersed in oil of some type with enough room to "float" in the hot oil. Cast-iron pans were a boon to improving this method, but in spite of helping keep the oil hot, there were drawbacks.

In a September 8, 1972 edition of the Arizona Daily Star, *Levy's Department Store advertised chimichanga demonstrations in the second-floor Gourmet Cookware section.*

In 1918, an invention changed commercial frying forever. J.C. Pitman & Sons was the earliest producer of commercial kitchen equipment. The company wanted to develop commercial equipment that would improve the methods used and set about researching how to do just that. It discovered that tiny particles of food settled to the bottom of a pan, where they often burned and ruined the oil and the food. They built a fryer in which tubes were used to heat the oil. The tubes ran through the center of the container and allowed for all those bits and pieces to fall below the tubes, which facilitated the entire process. It patented its invention and named it the Pitco Frialator. The product changed commercial frying forever.

In 1912, French chemist Louis-Camille Maillard wrote about his findings on how amino acids react with sugars at high temperatures, resulting in golden brown breads, French fries and, of course, chimichangas, although it's doubtful that Maillard ever imagined the dish. Other scientists studied his findings further, but to this day, it is called the "Maillard reaction."

It is doubtful that deep-fat fryers were common sights in early restaurant kitchens in Tucson, but by the late 1940s, they were almost a necessity. Improvements had been made. Fryers were both gas and electric, which allowed cooks to regulate the temperature, a vital element to the success of any fried food but especially for chimichangas. Also, they could cook more than one at a time.

If the oil is too hot, the tortilla burns on the outside, and the filling can be undercooked or even cold. If the oil is under temperature, then the food absorbs the oil and becomes greasy. The perfect temperature allows for the water in the food to evaporate, which means a golden, crisp surface and a preserved flavor.

Today, deep-frying at home is easier than ever thanks to tabletop deep-fryers. But using a heavy cast-iron pan can result in crispy chimis. Using the cast-iron pan also allows home cooks to cook more than one at a time—perfect when you're cooking for a crowd.

Tips for Making a Great Chimichanga

- Don't overfill the tortilla (but don't be stingy either). Place the filling about one quarter of the way from the bottom, but not all the way across. Fold the bottom over the filling and then fold in the sides. Slowly roll the tortilla, gently tucking the

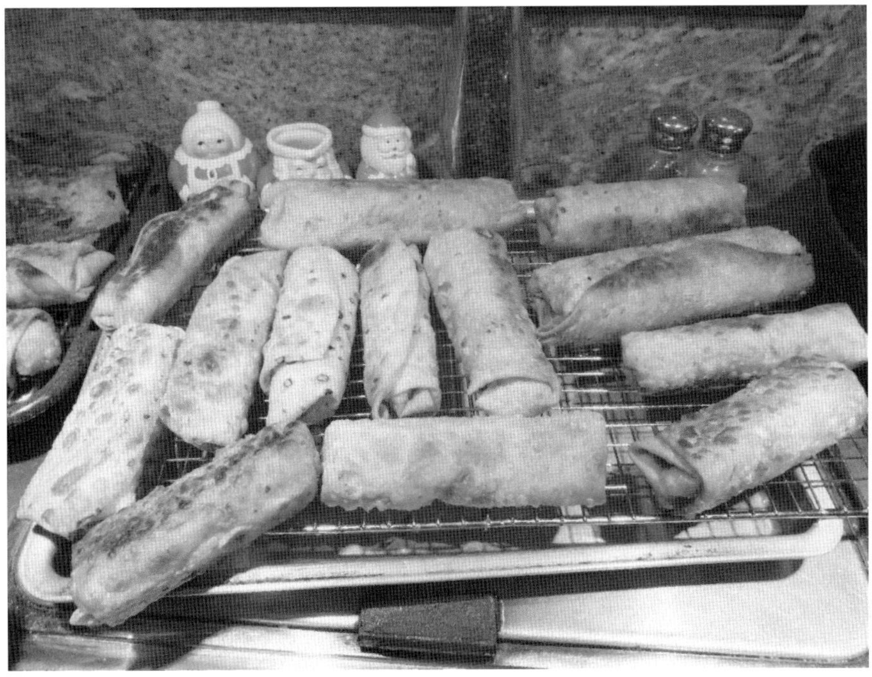

More delicious homemade chimis. *Author photo.*

tortilla around the filling, Fold over the top and secure with a toothpick. Then fry.

- Make sure the filling isn't too watery.
- The oil has to be at the right temperature. Too hot and the chimi will burn; too cool and the chimi will be greasy and the inside will absorb the flavor of the oil.
- The oil must be clean. You can reuse oil but strain all bits and pieces out of it.
- Don't overcrowd the food. This holds true whether you are deep-frying or pan-frying.
- If you are deep-frying, make sure there is enough oil in the pan to immerse the entire burro.
- Use toothpicks to secure the wrap (and don't forget to remove them before you serve).

Glossary of Fillings, Preparations and Other Pertinent Information Found in the Mexican Kitchen

ADOVADO (ADOBADO): New Mexican–style pork that has been marinated in red chile paste mixed with vinegar and various seasonings. You'll find it on menus in the Globe/Miami area and anywhere near the New Mexican state line.

AJO: garlic.

AL CARBON: meat cooked over charcoal or open flame.

AL PASTOR: pork that has been seasoned and then cooked on a vertical spit—when served, the meat is sliced into thin shreds, similar to shawarma; the style was adapted from Lebanese shepherds, hence "al pastor," who settled in central Mexico in the early twentieth century.

AL VAPOR: steamed.

ANAHEIM: large, green, mild pepper.

ANCHO: dried poblano.

ANTOJITOS: appetizers, sometimes called *botanas* (treats).

ARROZ: rice.

BARBACOA: meat (most often beef but sometimes goat or sheep), cooked slowly, traditionally steamed in an underground oven but today often cooked in a slow-cooker or the stovetop; originally from the Caribbean, barbacoa is more about how the food is prepared than the food itself.

BIRRIA: originally from the state of Jalisco, birria is traditionally a stew made with shredded goat meat, but these days it's more often made with beef; vinegar and spices are main ingredients.

BIZTEC: beef steak.

BOTANAS: "a surprise," but really an appetizer.

CALABACITAS: the term applies to both the vegetable—summer squash—and the dish itself, which is a blend of squash, corn and tomatoes.

CAMARONES: shrimp.

CARNE ASADA: grilled meat, usually on a flattop griddle.

CARNE SECA: beef, usually skirt steak, that has been seasoned with various dried herbs and spices and then hung to dry in the sun, resulting in a jerky-like texture; the meat is then shredded or chopped and reconstituted with tomatoes, chiles, onions and beef broth.

CARNITAS: pork, this time usually from the shoulder; the meat is seasoned, braised, pulled and then slow-cooked in the oven.

CHICHARRON: fried pork rinds.

CHILES: there are so many different kinds they almost deserve a stand-alone book; the most common are Anahiem, poblano, jalapeno, serrano and pasilla.

CHIPOTLE: jalapeños that have been dried and smoked.

CHORIZO: loose, highly seasoned sausage usually made with pork, although beef can be found at certain markets; usually it's mixed with eggs in breakfast chimis.

FRUTA: fruit.

FUNDIDO: a rich cheese sauce made from a mix of cheddar, Jack, Oaxacan and cream cheese and some type of meat (optional); in Tucson, it is usually served as an appetizer dip with chips, and in other parts of the state, fundido is used as a topping for chimis and other dishes.

GREEN CHILI (CHILE VERDE): made with either ground pork or chunks of pork, onions, chiles, tomatoes and seasonings.

HATCH CHILES: similar to Anaheim, these chiles can only originate from or around Hatch, New Mexico; they are renowned for their level of heat, versatility and flavor.

JALAPEÑO: a tiny, hot pepper.

LENGUA: tongue.

MACHACA: boiled beef that is then shredded and baked in a low oven to dry it out; prior to serving, the meat is tossed with oil, garlic, tomatoes, onions and chiles and crisped on a griddle.

MARISCOS: seafood.

MOLÉ: an intense blend of dried chiles, chocolate, nuts, seeds and seasonings, served most commonly blended with chicken.

NOPALES (TUNA): pads of the prickly pear cactus.

PASILLA: dark green, mild and often dried pepper.

PESCADO: fish.

PIBIL: pork that has been marinated in citrus, sometimes vinegar, and seasoned with annatto, which adds an orange hue as well as a peppery touch; the meat is then slow-cooked, traditionally in a pit.

PICADILLO: borrowed from Spain and found in other Latin countries and the Philippines, the Mexican version varies by region; ground beef, potatoes, tomatoes or tomato sauce, raisins, chiles and other spices are blended much like stew.

PICO DE GALLO: literally translated, it means "rooster's beak," but here it means a chunky salsa; it can also mean a spicy, chile powder-based seasoning sprinkled on large slices of fresh fruit cocktail.

PIERNA: leg of lamb; like chicken, the preparation depends on the cook.

PIPIAN: a type of mole made from pureed seed, usually pumpkin, and containing sesame seeds, peanuts, oil, onions, chiles, garlic, cloves, garlic and broth.

POBLANO: mild to medium in heat, these chiles are said to have origins in the state of Puebla.

POLLO: chicken; the preparation varies with the chef.

QUESO: cheese in any form, including queso fresco, sometimes called queso ranchero, which is similar to feta and is used mainly as a garnish, and queso asedero, which is similar to mozzarella and melts perfectly for fundido; purists believe that use of cheeses like cheddar or jack take away the authenticity of true Mexican food.

RANCHERO: mild salsa with the usual tomatoes, chiles, onions and garlic. Less chunky than pico de gallo.

RED CHILI (COLORADO): usually made with beef and seasoned with chiles, chile powder and other spices.

REFRIED BEANS (FRIJOLES REFRITOS); PINTO BEANS: the beans are cooked in water, drained and then pan fried in lard (more traditional) or vegetable shortening; during cooking, the beans are mashed, creating a smooth texture (some cooks add milk to aid the process).

RELLENO: the proper definition means stuffed, and you see this used most commonly with chiles stuffed with cheese, although creative chefs use meat; in some restaurants, a whole chile relleno is packed into a chimi.

SALSAS: like chiles, there are many types of salsa, although the basic recipe is chiles, tomatoes and onions, and the heat depends on the chile used; these days, fruit salsas are showing up in Mexican restaurants throughout Arizona and the rest of the United States.

SERRANO: small, dark green pepper, full of fire.

SOPAPILLAS: dough made from flour, water and baking powder, shaped into rounds and then fried in oil until golden brown, and it can be served sweet (honey, powdered sugar, etc.) or savory with red chili or other meats; it's also good plain hot out of the fryer.

TAMALE: an ancient food found in various forms throughout Mexico and Central and South America, corn meal (masa) is mixed with liquid (water, broth and so on) and fat (traditionally lard but in more modern times something more healthful) and then wrapped in a corn husk and steamed; the masa can be from yellow, white or blue corn.

TOMATILLO (SALSA VERDE): resembling tomatoes in shape with a papery covering, tomatillos are tiny and tart, which adds a nice counterpoint to the heat.

TOSTADA: a corn tortilla fried flat and topped with meats, fish or other protein; cheese; lettuce tomatoes; and salsa.

SPICY STUFF

A great source for authentic Mexican ingredients can be found in Tumacácori. The Santa Cruz Chili and Spice Company opened in 1943 almost directly across from the national park's entrance. The business is family owned and has a reputation of quality service and a long list of items for home and professional kitchens.

The aroma of chili powder scents the air as tourists and locals browse the store. The shelves are lined with salsas galore, packets and containers of Santa Cruz's famous chile paste and powders (in various levels of heat), spices, seasonings, house-made blends, masa flour, Southwest-related books and a table with a dozen samples of Santa Cruz salsas. Cookbooks, books on local history and geography, children's books, coloring books, kitchen utensils, pot holders and dish towels can also be found.

In the back are stacks of spice mixes that are created on site from chiles and other plants that are grown by the company on nearby farms.

Recipes

The following are a mix of restaurant recipes and home cook recipes. I have copied them from the cookbooks or websites (with permission), as I wanted to be authentic.

El Charro Machaca

Courtesy of Carlotta Flores.

A passable substitution for carne seca to make at home.
Yields 8 to 12 servings.

3 quarts of water
¼ cup garlic puree
4- to 6-pound eye of round, brisket or chuck, cut into several chunks

In an 8-quart stock pot, bring water to a boil. Add garlic paste and meat and bring to a boil. Skim off scum, reduce heat and simmer for about 2 hours or until meat is tender, removing scum frequently. Remove meat and set aside until meat is cool enough to handle. With fingers, shred meat along the grain into ½-inch-wide strips.

To brown and dry meat:
juice of 2 limes
¼ cup garlic puree

Preheat oven to 325 degrees. Spread shredded meat in a single layer on a large cookie sheet and sprinkle with lime juice and garlic puree. Roast meat until brown, about 15 minutes, stirring occasionally. Drain juices and reserve. At this point, the meat can be covered and refrigerated for later use.

To fry meat:
⅓ cup oil
1 cup chopped green chiles
½ teaspoon of salt, or to taste
½ teaspoon pepper
½ small white onion, sliced into rings
¼ cup garlic puree

shredded and roasted meat from above
2 tomatoes chopped

Heat oil in large skillet. Sauté chiles with salt and pepper. Add onion and sauté briefly and then add the garlic puree. Add meat and tomatoes, stirring over medium heat to brown. If it is too dry, add the reserved juices. Use in chimis, tacos, enchiladas and more.

To make garlic puree:
Peel 8 whole heads of garlic by smashing the cloves with the side of a wide knife. Remove peel. Put garlic in blender with 2 cups of water and puree. Drain if necessary and save in a covered container in the refrigerator.

Pancho's Green Chili

Courtesy Frank Gonzales, Mi Cocona de Amor.

This is the green chili that inspired Ken Lamberton to travel Arizona in search of the perfect chimichanga. Frank Gonzales III, grandson of the original Pancho (Frank Gonzales) and son of Frank Sr., uses this recipe at his restaurant, Mi Cocina de Amor, in Charleston, West Virginia. He noted that at the restaurant, his grandmother and mother probably used beef, but he says either meat works.

32 ounces chicken stock
1 cup cilantro, finely chopped
10 cloves garlic (7 chopped finely)
14 to 16 fresh Anaheim green chiles (Hatch for more heat), about 6 cups
3 pounds pork shoulder or inside top round
2 large onions, diced
salt and pepper
1 tablespoons oregano
32 ounces tomatoes

Keep about 12 ounces stock, the cilantro and 3 cloves of garlic aside. Roast chiles however able (grill or oven). Peel and remove some seeds (optional). Keep 4 aside. Brown cubed pork with oil; set aside. Add onion and garlic to pan with meat drippings. Sweat until translucent and add stock. Add salt, pepper and oregano. Bring to boil and stir and simmer for a few minutes. Combine remaining stock, cilantro, 4 chiles and garlic in blender and run until smooth. Combine to thicken and add tomatoes, reduce heat and cover. Cook for 2 to 3 hours until super tender.

Macayo's Chicken Poblano Chimi
(One of the Special Chimichangas from the Chimi Fiesta Menu)

Courtesy of Macayo Family Restaurants.

1 each roasted poblano, sliced lengthwise
1 each flour tortilla, 13-inch
5 ounces shredded chicken
3 ounces Macayo's Red Enchilada Sauce
1 ounce Macayo's Famous Baja Sauce
¼ ounce shredded jack cheese
tomatoes, diced, as needed

Place the sliced poblano in the center of a 13-inch tortilla and then spoon 5 ounces of shredded chicken on top of poblano. Fold other half of poblano over shredded chicken. Roll the tortilla burrito style, enclosing the filling and sealing the tortilla ends. Place prepared chimichanga into the basket of the deep-fryer, folds down, to prevent opening during frying. Deep-fry chimichanga to a golden brown and then allow grease to drain. Top chimi with 3 ounces of Macayo's Red Enchilada Sauce. Spoon 1 ounce of Macayo's Famous Baja Sauce in the middle of the chimichanga. Top with ¼ ounce shredded jack cheese and diced tomatoes.

Gordo's Ground Beef Chimichanga

Courtesy of Marguerite Brown and Julie Valenzuela.

1 pound ground beef
½ cup chopped onion
½ cup chopped green bell pepper
1 small can tomato sauce
granulated garlic
salt and pepper to taste

12-inch flour tortillas
canola or vegetable oil

In a large sauce pan, brown the ground beef, add onion, green pepper and tomato sauce. Season with garlic, salt and pepper to taste. Let simmer until ground beef is cooked through. Turn off heat and let cook down. Add some of mixture to tortilla and roll as a burro, making sure the ends are enclosed. Fry in oil at 375 degrees until tortillas are browned and crispy. Top with salsa, shredded cheese and guacamole and sour cream if desired.

Pork Adovada, Los Dos Molino

Courtesy Victoria Chavez and Los Dos Molinos.

This makes a lot of food. It hasn't been adjusted for a home kitchen, but it will freeze well for later use.

6 to 8 pounds pork loin, cut into 2- to 3-inch cubes
½ cup New Mexico powder chile
½ cup New Mexico chile flakes
2 tablespoons oregano
2 tablespoons garlic salt
2 tablespoons cumin
2 tablespoons fresh garlic, crushed
2 tablespoons black pepper
2 Spanish onions, chopped
2 cups broth

Put all ingredients in a Dutch oven. Cook uncovered for 4 hours. Turn off heat and check for tenderness but do not stir.

Vincent on Camelback's Lobster Chimichanga

Courtesy of Vincent Guerithault.

Cilantro Beurre Blanc
1 cup white wine
1 cup white wine vinegar

1 tablespoon chopped shallots
1 tablespoon heavy cream
1 pound unsalted butter, cut into eight cubes
¾ cup chopped cilantro

¾ pound fresh lobster meat
1 large leek, white part diced
¼ cup heavy cream
salt and white pepper
4 flour tortillas, 7 inches diameter
2 ounces goat cheese, cut into four portions
2 cups vegetable shortening

Put the wine, vinegar and shallots in a skillet and reduce the mixture over moderate heat until the liquid is completely gone and only the shallots remain. Whisk in the cream and softened butter, one cube at a time. Add the chopped cilantro. Serve the sauce hot but do not allow it to boil.

Blanch the lobster meat for 2 minutes in boiling water and set it aside. Blanch the diced leek for 1 to 2 minutes to soften. Pour the cream into a heavy pan and cook it over medium-high heat for several minutes until it thickens; add the blanched leek and season to taste. Allow the mixture to cool.

To assemble, spread the center of each tortilla with a quarter of the reduced cream and leek mixture. Place a portion of the goat cheese and a quarter of the lobster meat slightly off-center on each tortilla. Fold two sides of the tortillas over the filling, roll them up tightly and secure each roll with a toothpick. Heat the shortening to about 365 degrees Fahrenheit in a deep pot and deep-fry the chimichangas for 3 to 4 minutes, or until they are cooked through and a deep golden brown. Drain briefly on paper towels. Serve the chimichangas with cilantro beurre blanc.

Calabacitas Breakfast Chimichanga

Courtesy of my kitchen.

You won't find these chimis on any menu (it's an original), but they make an ideal dish for a company breakfast. Make the filling the

MAYO ON A CHIMI?

Although it isn't common north of the border, people do serve mayo on chimichangas. In an article in the September 1997 issue of *Arizona Highways*, Leo Banks quoted a Tucson restaurant owner who ate a chimi with mayo in a little restaurant near downtown Tucson in 1959.

When the *Arizona Star* ran an article called "Tucson in 100 Objects," a reader responded with his story of eating chivichangas in a bus station in Imuris, Mexico. The shape was different, but the item was served with mayo and shredded cabbage. This was in the 1970s, but in researching Mexican chimis, *Star* food writer Andi Berlin visited the bus station and found the same dish served the same way. Finally, on the Spanish-language Wikipedia page for chimichanga (where they mention two other names for chimis, *chimijuanga* and *chanchorro*), the writer noted that in parts of Mexico, chimis are served in different ways and, in Sonora, "are commonly accompanied with mayonnaise and a salsa made of chopped tomatoes, chile, cilantro, and chiltepin; also giving a touch of lemon."

We've never experienced mayo on chimis, but when we do, more research will be conducted. You might want to try mayo on your homemade chimis.

night before, and when your guests wake up, start making the chimis or make the chimis at night and reheat in the oven in the morning as your guests roll out of bed.

5 ears of fresh corn
2 large zucchinis
2 large tomatoes
1 large can of green chiles
6 eggs
¼ cup water
½ cup of flour
½ cup sharp cheddar cheese, grated

salt and pepper, to taste
6 medium or large flour tortillas

Remove corn from the cob. Chop zucchinis and tomatoes into half-inch pieces. Chop chiles. Mix all together in a large bowl. In a second bowl, beat eggs until light and fluffy; add water and sprinkle in flour, incorporating a little at a time to avoid lumps. The batter should be very thin. Add vegetables to eggs and then add half of the cheese. Mix together. Add salt and pepper to taste. Pour in a greased baking dish and sprinkle with the rest of the cheese. Bake at 350 degrees until the eggs set, about 30 minutes. Let cool; if preparing chimis in the morning, refrigerate overnight. When cooled, divide the eggs into six even amounts. Fill the tortillas with egg mixture, shape chimi and fry as usual. Serve with your favorite salsa.

Enchilada Sauce, Red

Courtesy of my kitchen.

1 clove of garlic, minced
½ teaspoon cumin
½ teaspoon, dried oregano
4 tablespoons vegetable oil
2 tablespoons all-purpose flour
5 tablespoons good quality chili powder
3 cups of chicken broth

In a heavy skillet over medium heat, toast the garlic, cumin and oregano in vegetable oil, stirring to ensure that the garlic doesn't overcook, about 1 minute. Add flour a little at a time and continue stirring until the flour taste cooks out, 3 to 4 minutes. Add chili powder and toast about 1 minute. Add chicken broth and bring it to a boil. Cook on low for about 15 minutes, stirring constantly until sauce achieves a smooth texture. If the sauce seems too thick or dry, add more broth a little at a time.

Casa Serrano's Mexican Style Rice

Courtesy of Anthony Serrano.

According to Anthony Serrano, the secret to great Mexican-style rice, which is fluffy and light, is a method called pearling, aka pilaf style. The rice is sautéed in oil and butter first. During this step, make sure each grain of rice is thoroughly coated until shiny.

1 tablespoon olive oil
1 tablespoon butter
⅛ cup of diced onion
2 cloves of minced garlic
1 cup of jasmine rice
⅛ cup diced tomatoes
1 jalapeño finely diced (optional)
2 cups chicken stock
sea salt and pepper

Heat oil and butter in skillet and sauté onion and garlic for 2 to 3 minutes. Add uncooked rice and sauté for several minutes or until rice begins to brown slightly. Add tomatoes, jalapeño and chicken stock. Add salt and pepper and cover with a lid. Reduce heat to slow simmer and cook for 20 minutes. Lightly fluff rice with fork and serve.

Refried Beans

Makes 8 to 10 side servings or filling for 4 to 6 chimis depending on size of tortilla (more if you're adding additional fillings).

3 cups dried pinto beans
water
½ cup of lard or bacon drippings
4 cloves of garlic, smashed
½ white onion, finely chopped
whole milk or evaporated milk
¾ cup shredded cheddar cheese (or Monterrey Jack)
salt and pepper to taste

Place beans in deep pot and cover generously with water. Bring to a boil and then reduce heat to low. Cook slowly until beans are tender (2 to 3 hours). Reserve the cooking liquid. Over low heat in a large, heavy skillet, heat the lard or bacon drippings. Sauté garlic and onions until soft. Add ¼ of beans and begin to mash. Continue adding cooked beans until smooth. Add cooking liquid a little at a time as needed to keep mixture moist and smooth. You can add a splash of milk or evaporated milk as well. Stir in cheese until melted. Season to taste, but go light on salt as lard and drippings add salt naturally. Serve hot or reheat later.

Salsa

This recipe comes from the Mexico Inn, where I worked many years ago. The Mexico Inn is now closed. During my time there, I learned how to make this salsa. Regrettably, even though we made a huge batch of this salsa practically every day, I don't remember the exact recipe, but this is close.

1 large can of crushed tomatoes
¼ to ½ cup dried red pepper flakes
2 to 3 scallions, cut into small rings
2 tablespoons oregano
2 cloves of garlic, minced
handful of fresh cilantro, chopped
salt and pepper

Mix all ingredients and serve.

EPILOGUE

ARIZONA'S CULINARY WONDER

Chimis are what makes us who we are. They were invented here.
We are the chimichanga.
—Ken Lamberton, author of
Chasing Arizona: One Man's Yearlong Obsession
with the Grand Canyon State

Of course, writing about chimis meant eating chimis, and I did eat a lot of them—not great for the waistline, but in all that eating, I learned one thing: not all chimis are alike. Certainly the basics are the same: a flour tortilla wrapped around some type of filling and then fried. But I ate chimis that were fat and short and chimis that were long and tubular. I ate chimis that were fried and chimis that were grilled. I ate chimis that were crackling crisp and others with hidden layers of tender tortillas. I ate chimis covered with enchilada sauce, cheese, guacamole, sour cream and even tzatziki sauce. I ate chimis served simply, with the only embellishments being lettuce and a smattering of salsa. There wasn't one bad chimi in the whole bunch, but there were some outstanding ones. And I can't tell you which one I liked best.

I learned that depending on which part of Arizona you are in, chimis differ greatly. The chimis in Tucson and Phoenix are gigantic because they are made with large, thin tortillas that can be hard to come by as you head north, east or west. While fillings in Tucson are more traditional, seafood, stews and meats from other cultures show up as you head north, east and west. The chimis get smaller and the toppings also change. As an example, fundido sauce is extremely popular statewide except for in Tucson, where the only way fundido is served is as an appetizing dip. And cream sauces are as varied as the restaurants that offer them.

I grew to admire the creativity of chefs and cooks throughout the state and to appreciate the hard work it takes to run a successful restaurant. The great chimichanga debate will no doubt rage on. As stated earlier, we take no sides in the many stories about the origins of chimichangas. But even with all those various claims, Arizonans take great pride in the fact that it was here that someone, somewhere in the state put a chimichanga on a restaurant menu. From there, the world took to chimichangas like few other foods.

Carlotta Flores said it best: "I feel privileged to be the one that has been able to tell the story of the chimichanga." I second that sentiment.

ADDRESSES

Southern Arizona

TUCSON

El Charro
https://www.elcharrocafe.com
311 North Court Avenue
Tucson, AZ 85701
520-622-1922

7725 North Oracle
Oro Valley, AZ 85704
520-229-1922

6910 East Sunrise
Tucson, AZ 85750
520-514-1922

Sir Veza's
https://www.sirvezas.com
220 West Wetmore Road
Tucson, AZ 85705
520-888-TACO (8226)

PHOENIX AREA

Sir Veza's
3111 West Chandler Boulevard
Chandler, AZ 85226
480-899-TACO (8226)

Mi Nidito
http://www.minidito.net
1813 South Fourth Avenue
Tucson, AZ 85712
520-622-5081

Casa Molina
https://casamolina.com
6225 East Speedway Boulevard
Tucson, AZ 85712
520-886-5468

Casa Molina del Norte
http://casamolinadelnorte.com
3001 North Campbell Avenue
Tucson, AZ 85719
520-795-7593

Casa Molina
4240 East Grant Road
Tucson, AZ 85712
520-326-6663

El Molinito
http://www.elmolinitos.com
5380 East Twenty-Second Street
Tucson, AZ 85711
520-747-9162

3675 West Ina Road
Tucson, AZ 85741
520-744-1188

2323 North Pantano Road
Tucson, AZ 85715
520-885-0055

10180 North Oracle Road
Oro Valley, AZ 85704
520-268-8180

El Minuto Café
https://www.elminutotucson.com
354 South Main Avenue
Tucson, AZ 85701
520-882-4145

Club 21
http://www.club21restaurant.com
2920 North Oracle Road
Tucson AZ 85705
520-622-3092

El Saguarito
www.elsaguarito.com
3535 East Fort Lowell Road
520-297-1264

La Indita
http://lainditarestauranttucson.com/6842
622 North Fourth Avenue
Tucson AZ, 85705
520-792-0523

Tortilleria Arevalo
www.tortilleriaarevalo.com
520-954-7782

Rosa's Mexican Food
https://www.tucsonmexicanrestaurant.com
1750 East Fort Lowell Road #164, Suite 164
Tucson, AZ 85719
520-325-0362

TUMACÁCORI

Wisdom's Café
http://www.wisdomscafe.com
1931 East Frontage Road
Tumacácori, AZ 85640
520-398-2397

Santa Cruz Chili & Spice Company
http://www.santacruzchili.com
1868 East Frontage Road
Tumacácori, AZ 85640
520-398-2591

BENSON

Mi Casa
https://www.facebook.com/Mi-Casa-Restaurant
723 West Fourth Street
Benson, AZ
520-245-0343

DOUGLAS

Casa Segovia, Gadsden Hotel
https://thegadsdenhotel.com/casa-segovia
1046 G Avenue
Douglas, AZ 85607
520-364-1169

BISBEE

Santiago's
http://www.santiagosmexican.com
1 Howell Avenue
520-432-1910

PHOENIX

Macayo
www.macayo.com
6012 West Bell Road
Glendale, AZ 85308
602-298-8080

Woody's Macayo
3815 North Central Avenue
Phoenix, AZ 85012
602-264-6141

7829 West Thomas Road
Phoenix, AZ 85033
623-873-0313

1474 North Litchfield Road
Goodyear, AZ 85338
623-209-7000

Depot Cantina
300 South Ash Avenue
Tempe, AZ 85281
480-966-6677

920 South Dobson Road
Mesa, AZ 85202
480-820-0237

12637 South Forty-Eighth Street
Ahwautokee, AZ 85044
480-598-5101

15565 West Bell Road
Surprise, AZ 85374
623-214-5950

Mi Patio
http://www.mipatioaz.com/menu.htm
3347 North Seventh Avenue
Phoenix, AZ 85013
620-277-4831

Aunt Chilada's
https://www.auntchiladas.com
7330 North Dreamy Draw Drive
Phoenix, AZ 85020
602-944-1286

Los Dos Molinos
http://losdosmolinosphoenix.com
1044 East Camelback Road
Phoenix, AZ 85014
602-528-3535

8046 South Central Avenue
Phoenix, AZ 85042
602-243-9113

260 South Alma School Road
Mesa, AZ 85210
480-969-7475

Rosita's Place
http://www.therositasplace.com
2310 East McDowell Road
Phoenix, AZ 85006
602-244-9779

La Pinata
http://lapinatarestaurantaz.com
5521 North Seventh Avenue
Phoenix, AZ 85013
602-279-1763

Xavier's Casa Reynoso
3701 East Southern Avenue
Mesa, AZ
480-860-8005

Carolina's
https://carolinasmexicanfood.com
1202 East Mohave Street
Phoenix, AZ 85022
602-252-1503

2126 East Cactus Road
Phoenix, AZ
602-275-8231

Vincent on Camelback
https://www.vincentsoncamelback.com
3930 North Camelback Road
Phoenix, AZ 85028
602-224-0225

Ryu Sushi
http://www.ryusushi.com/menu.html
2512 South Val Vista Drive
Gilbert, AZ 85295
480-857-3999

Mango's Mexican Café
https://www.mangosmexicancafe.com
44 West Main Street
Mesa, AZ 85201
480-464-5700

Original Blue Adobe Grille
http://www.originalblueadobe.com
144 North Country Club Drive
Mesa, AZ 85201
480-962-1000

Anaya's Fresh Mexican
http://anayasfreshmexicanrestaurant.com
5830 Thunderbird Road
Glendale, AZ 85306
602-559-4377

Valle Luna
http://valleluna.com
3336 West Bell Road
Phoenix, AZ 85053
602-993-3108

16048 North Cave Creek Road
Phoenix, AZ 85032
602-867-9100

The Boardwalk at Anderson Spring
1949 North Ray Road
Chandler, AZ 85234
480-786-3100

Ocotillo Restaurant
https://www.ocotillophx.com
3243 North Third Street
Phoenix, AZ 85012
602-687-9080

CASA GRANDE

Eva's Fine Mexican
http://www.evasmexicanfood.com
665 North Pinal Avenue
Casa Grande, AZ 85722
520-836-0016

Anaya's Fresh Mexican Restaurant
http://anayasfreshmexicanrestaurant.com
2876 North Pinal Avenue
Casa Grande, AZ
520-788-6979

Little Sombrero
419 East Florence Boulevard
Casa Grande, AZ 8522
520-836-2567

Northern Arizona

FLAGSTAFF

MartAnne's Burrito Palace
https://www.facebook.com/MartAnnes
112 West Historic Route 66
Flagstaff, AZ 86001
928-773-4701

Salsa Brava
http://www.salsabravaflagstaff.com
2220 East Route 66
Flagstaff, AZ 86004
928-779-5293

Agave Mexican Restaurant
http://www.agaveflagstaff.com
1580 East Route 66
Flagstaff, AZ 86001
928-774-1429

El Tapatio
http://tapatiorestaurants.com
2004 East Historic Route 66
Flagstaff, AZ 86004
928-774-3530

SEDONA

El Rincon Restaurante Mexicano
ElRinconRestaurant.com
336 State Route 179
Sedona, AZ 863336
928-282-4648

Javalina Cantina
www.javelinacantina.com
671 Highway 179, Suite BF
Sedona, AZ 86004
928-282-1313

SHOW LOW

Mateo's Mexican Grill and Cantina
https://www.facebook.com/MateosMexicanGrillandCantina
4817 South White Mountain Road
Show Low, AZ 85901
928-537-8828

PAGE

El Tapatio
http://tapatiorestaurants.com
25 Lake Havasu Road
Page, AZ 86040
928-645-4055

KINGMAN

Oyster's
http://www.oystersaz.com
2906 Andy Devine Avenue
Kingman, AZ 86401
928-753-2030

PAYSON

El Rancho
https://www.elranchopayson.com
200 South Beeline Highway
Payson, AZ 85541
928-474-3111

GLOBE-MIAMI-MAMMOTH

Chalo's Casa Reynoso
902 East Ash Street
Globe, AZ 85501
928-425-0515

J&R'a El Rey
999 North Broad Street 85501
Globe, AZ 85501
928-425-8154

Guayo's on the Trail
http://guayosrestaurants.com
Highway 188 Apache Trail
Miami, AZ 85539
928-425-9969

La Casita East
1960 East Ash Street
Globe, AZ 85501
928-425-2700

La Casita Café
400 Highway AZ 77
Mammoth, AZ
520-487-9980

Irene's Real Mexican Food
1601 East Ash Street
Globe, AZ
628-425-7904

Guayo's El Rey
http://guayosrestaurants.com
716 Sullivan Street
Miami, AZ
928-473-9960

Arizona's West Coast

YUMA

Blaisdell Steakhouse & Mexican Food
http://www.blaisdellsteakhouse.com
11411 South Fortuna Road
Yuma, AZ 85367
928-342-8398

Cretin's
http://chretins.com
928 East Sixteenth Street
Yuma, AZ 85635
928-782-1291

BULLHEAD CITY

El Palacio Family Restaurants
http://epfamilyrestaurants.com
1885 Highway 95
Bullhead City, AZ 86441
928-763-2494

LAKE HAVASU

El Palacios
http://epfamilyrestaurants.com
150 Swanson Avenue
Lake Havasu City, AZ 86403
928-854-5500

Javalina Cantina
http://javelinacantina.com
1420 McCulloch Boulevard
Lake Havasu, AZ 86403
928-855-8226

PARKER

Maya Restaurant & Sports Cantina
http://www.mayascantina.com
621 West Riverside Drive
Parker, AZ 85344
928-575-4949

FORT MOHAVE

El Palacios
http://epfamilyrestaurants.com
5230 Arizona 95
Fort Mohave, AZ 86426
928-768-1881

PRESCOTT

Arturo's
http://arturosaz.com
Arturo's Mexican Restaurant—Prescott
503 Miller Valley Road
Prescott, AZ 86301
928-445-5787

Arturo's Mexican Restaurant—Chino Valley
900 South Highway 89
Chino Valley, AZ 86323
928-636-0221

Fiesta Mexican Grill
http://fiestamexicangrillroute66.com
3050 North Windsong Drive
Prescott Valley, AZ 86314
928-759-7086

WILLIAMS

Fiesta Mexican Grill
http://fiestamexicangrillroute66.com
122 West Historic Route 66
928-635-1146
Williams, AZ 96046

DEWEY

Puerto Vallerta Family Mexican Restaurant
11901 AZ 69
Dewey, AZ 86327
928-772-4460

GRAHAM COUNTY

Casa Manana
https://www.thecasamanana.com
502 South First Avenue
Safford, AZ 85546
928-428-3170

El Charro
http://www.elcharrogrill.com
601 West Main Street
Safford, AZ 85546
928-428-4134

La Paloma
http://lapalomarestaurant.net
218 Clifton Street
Solomon, AZ 85551
928-428-2094

El Coronado
409 West Main Street
Safford, AZ 85548
928-428-7755

GiMee's
AZ 75, Mile Post 395
York, AZ 85534
928-687-1517

Isabel's South of the Border
https://www.facebook.com/IsabelsMexicanFood
135 East Maley Street
Willcox, AZ 85643
520-253-0859

La Unica Tortilliaria y Taqueria
https://www.facebook.com/pg/Tortilleria-Taqueria-La-Unica
142 North Haskell Avenue
Willcox, AZ 85643
520-384-0010

Manor House & Rock n' Horse Saloon
http://visitsaffordmanorhouse.com
415 East US 70
Safford, AZ
928-428-7148

Mechy's Mexican Food
http://mechysmexican.com
750 West Fifth Street
Safford, AZ 85545
928-348-9711

Michelle's Bar & Grill
450 Highway 191
Morenci, AZ 85540
928-865-9050

Taco Taste
https://www.facebook.com/Tacotaste
1827 Thatcher Boulevard
Safford, AZ
928-428-3414

Taylor Freeze
https://www.facebook.com/pg/PimaTaylorFreeze
225 West Center Street
Pima, AZ 85543
928-485-2661

West Virginia

Mi Cocina de Amor
https://www.wvmexicanfood.com
711 Bigley Avenue
Charleston, WV 25302
304-205-5461

Nevada

Macayo's
1741 East Charleston Boulevard
Las Vegas, NV 89104
702-382-5605

8245 West Sahara Avenue
Las Vegas, NV 89117
702-360-8210

El Palacio Family Restaurants
http://epfamilyrestaurants.com
1650 South Casino Drive
Laughlin, NV 89029
702-299-0817

Hecho in Vegas
https://www.mgmgrand.com
3799 South Las Vegas Boulevard
Las Vegas, NV 89109
702-891-3200

BIBLIOGRAPHY

Adams-Ockrassa, Suzanne. "Agave Brings Taste, Flavor of Mexico to Flagstaff." *Arizona Daily Sun*, January 11, 2015.

Anable, Luke. "A Page of Bisbee." *Edible Baja Arizona*, November 2016.

Arizona Highways. "Best Restaurants—50 of Our Favorites." 2015.

Arizona Republic. "Macayo Owned by Johnsons." October 21, 1959.

———. Rita Riddle-Wilson obituary. January 2009.

Arizona's Salsa Trail. Kirkland, AZ: Jamax Publishers, 2009.

Arizona Star. "Tucson in 100 Objects." Letter to the writer, April 22, 2014.

Armato, Dominic. "Dominic Armato Searches for the Best Chimichanga, from Dry to Wet, Fab to Fat." *Arizona Republic*, n.d.

———. "Ocotillo Blooms." *Arizona Republic*, June 15, 2016.

———. "10 Best Restaurants in Arizona Known for Their Classic Culinary History." *Arizona Republic*, October 22, 2017.

Arrellano, Gustavo. "In Praise of Flour Tortillas, an Unsung Jewel of the U.S.-Mexico Borderlands." *The New Yorker*, January 13, 2018.

———. "Was the Chimichanga Invented by the Chinese in Mexico?" *OC Weekly*, April 29, 2014.

Attoun, Marti. "Who Invented the Banana Split?" American Profile, June 4, 2009. americanprofile.com.

Auslander, Edith Sayre. "Mexican Food Row." *Arizona Daily Star*, October 30, 1977.

Bagwell, Keith. "Alaskan Caribou Beats 4 Other Game Entrants in Cook-Off." *Arizona Daily Star*, January 24. 1988.

Balint, Vicki Louk. "Leevon Guerithault—Everything but Cooking." *Raising Arizona Kids*, November 1, 2012.

Banks, Leo. "The Chimi that Ate Tucson." *Tucson Weekly*, 1997.

———. "The Great Chimichanga Quest." *Arizona Highways*, September 1997.

Bilker, Molly. "La Pinata Moves to '21st Century' Digs in Phoenix." *Arizona Highways*, November 11, 2015.

Bisbee Chamber of Commerce. https://bisbeearizona.com.

Boan, Christopher. "For the Kids, New Tubac Ballpark Almost Ready." *Sahuarita Sun*, March 30, 2015.

Bonan, Max. "5 Things You Didn't Know About Hatch Chiles." Food and Wine. foodandwine.com.

Bonuccelli, Dominic A.Z. "What Makes Your Tortillas the Best in Town." *Edible Baja Arizona*, March/April 2015.

Booth, George C. *The Food & Drink of Mexico.* Los Angeles: Ward Ritchie Press, 1964.

Boran, Rebecca. "Chimichangas a Tasty Mystery." *Arizona Daily Star*, April 30, 2003.

Buchanan, Nikki. "Best Restaurants." *Arizona Highways*, April 2008–12.

Burch, Cathelina E. "Micha's Rolls Out Food Truck While Waiting for Fire Repairs." *Arizona Daily Star*, June 2, 2018.

———. "Micha's Will Rebuild After Fire Devastates Longtime Tucson Restaurant, Family Says." *Arizona Daily Star*, April 16, 2018.

Burros, Marion. "On the Trail of the Tortilla: All Trails Lead to Tucson." *New York Times*, August 15, 1990.

Cole, Dana. "Mi Casa Chamber's Spotlight Business for April." *Benson News-Sun*, April 15, 2014.

———. "Mi Casa Quickly Becoming the Taste of Cochise County." *Bisbee News-Sun*, July 22, 2014.

Connelly, Rita. *Historic Restaurants of Tucson.* Charleston, SC: The History Press, 2018.

———. *Lost Restaurants of Tucson*. Charleston, SC: The History Press, 2015.

The Cooking Channel. "Townie Treats." *Food: Fact or Fiction*, April 29, 2018.

———. *Bloodlines.* May 2018.

Corcoran, Penelope. "Carolina's Tortillas Prove Flat-Out Best." *Arizona Republic*, April 2. 1996.

Cordova, Randy. "Claiming the Chimi." *Arizona Republic*, n.d.

Cross, Malcolm. "Get to Know 3 R's; Rich, Reliable, Real." *AZ Business Gazette*, May 1, 1997.

Cusimano, Laura. "The Essential Mexican Restaurant Dish Best Ordered with a To-Go Box." *Phoenix New Times*, January 28, 2017.

Dark Haunts. "Aunt Chiladas: Phoenix, Arizona." http://darkhaunts.com/ArizonaGhostStories/AuntChiladas.htm.

Delgado, Grace Peña. "Of Kith and Kin: Land, Leases and Guanxi in Tucson's Chinese and Mexican Communities, 1880s–1920s." *Journal of Arizona History* (Spring 2005).

Downing, Renee. "Tucson's Native Cuisine." *Tucson Weekly*, July, 26, 2007.

Duarte, Carmen. "Casa Molina, Sister's Cooking Blazed New Frontier." *Arizona Daily Star*, April 30, 1981.

———. "Richard Mariscal, 64, Micha's Restaurant's Beloved Manager, Dies." *Arizona Daily Star*, September 27, 2013.

El Charro Café. www.elcharrocafe.com.

El Minuto Café. https://www.elminutotucson.com.

Escarcega, Patricia. "The Landmark New Mexico–Style Restaurant that's Made for Chileheads." *Phoenix New Times*, April 23, 2018.

———. "Ocotillo in Central Phoenix Is an Ode to Arizona Showcasing Local Ingredients—and Local Talent." *Phoenix New Times*, May 4, 2016.

Flores, Carlotta Dunn, with Susan Lyons Anderson. *Favorite Recipes: El Charro Café and the Story of Its Colorful Past.* Tucson, AZ: El Charro Café, 1989.

Flores, Carlotta. *El Charro Café: The Tastes & Traditions of Tucson.* Tucson, AZ: Fisher Books, 1998.

Gay, Gerald. "Micha's Started as a One-Room Affair." *Arizona Daily Star*, February 12, 2009.

Gourmet. "America's Legendary Restaurants—El Charro." October 2008.

Greenberg, Laura. "Baja Eats." *Edible Baja Arizona*, March/April 2016.

Gullette, A.V. "Luck Is Spice of Woody's Life." *Arizona Republic*, November 10, 1968.

———. "$9 Million Enterprise Built on Boom on Mexican Foods." *Arizona Republic*, May 29, 1997.

Hahnfield, Lillian. "Let's Make It Official: Arizona Needs a State Food." *Phoenix New Times*, February 9, 2012.

———. "Macayo's and Others Make Deep-Fried Push for Chimichanga as State Food." *Phoenix New Times*, February 20, 2012.

Happe, Marguerite. "Dishing Up History." *Tucson Lifestyle* (Winter/Spring 2016–17).

Henderson, John. "We All Win as Chimichanga War Rages On." *Denver Post*, January 24, 2007.

Henry, Bonnie. "Mission Only One Reason to Visit." *Arizona Daily Star*, May 16, 2010.

Hwang, Kelli. "Macayo's Owners Are Opening Woody's." *Arizona Republic*, October 27, 2017.

Internet Movie Database. "Anthony Serrano." https://www.imdb.com/name/nm9678056.

Jarman, Max. "Macayo's Matriarch Leaves Legacy of Good Service." *Arizona Republic*, February 8, 2011.

Jarolim, Edie. "Arizona's Historical Mexican Restaurants." Visit Arizona, August 2, 2011. VisitArizona.com.

———. "A Food and a Family Force." *BizTucson* (February 26, 2015).

Jones, Carrie. "Whoever Invented the French Dip, We Love It." Food and Wine, June 22, 2017. foodandwine.com.

Kelley, Cary. "Who Invented the Chimichanga?" Zocalo Public Square, May 1, 2015. http://www.zocalopublicsquare.org/2015/05/01/who-invented-the-chimichanga/ideas/nexus.

Kramer, Kelly. "Hot Stuff." *Arizona Highways*, April 2012.

Lacey, Mark. "Arizonans Vie to Claim Cross-Cultural Fried Food." *New York Times*, November 15, 2011.

Lamberton, Ken. *Chasing Arizona: One Man's Year Long Obsession with the Grand Canyon State*. Tucson: University of Arizona Press, 2015.

Laudig, Michelle. "Chimi Eat World." *Phoenix New Times*, November 22, 2007.

Leach, Anita Mahante. "La Pinata's Recipes Are All in the Family." *Arizona Republic*, July 22, 2000.

Lehrman, Adam. "If You Like Really Chimichangas, Then View the Original Gordo's Commercials." Tucson Foodie, September 2, 2015. tucsonfoodie.com.

Le Moin, Leah. "Chimi Chimi Bang Bang." *Phoenix Magazine* (February 2016).

Lobaco, Julia. "Family Is Main Ingredient for Success of Mexican Restaurant in Phoenix." *Arizona Republic*, June 14, 1985.

The Longhorn Restaurant. http://bignosekates.info/longhorn.html.

Los Compadres. loscompadres.com.

"Macayo Founder, Woody Johnson." Obituary, *Arizona Republic*, September 14, 1999.

Mateo, Merra. "Tales of the Chimichanga Origin." Maria-online.com.

Melton, Drew, producer. *Un Dia a la Vez*, 2017.

Mexican Food and Mexican Recipes. mexgrocer.com.

Miller, Tom, and Peter Hamill. *Revenge of the Saguaro: Offbeat Travels through the Southwest.* N.p.: Cinco Punto Press, 2010.

Mi Nidito menui. http://www.minidito.net.

Miranda, Natalie. "Casa Reynoso Tempe vs. Casa Reynoso Chandler: Battle of the Restaurants." *Phoenix New Times*, March 27, 2014.

Montague, Prosper. *The New LaRousse Gastronomique.* New York: Crown Publishing, n.d.

Myal, Susan. *Tucson's Mexican Restaurants: Repasts, Recipes and Remembrances.* Tucson: University of Arizona Press, 1997.

National Park Service. "Tumacácori National Historic Park." https://www.nps.gov/tuma/index.htm.

Naylor, Roger. "Arizona's Best Mexican Restaurants: Tacos and More from Flagstaff to Tucson to Yuma." AZ Central, April 30, 2018. azcentral.com.

Nothaft, Mark. "Casa Reynoso Worth the Trip to Mill Avenue." *Arizona Republic*, February 14, 2015.

The Original Carolina's Mexican Food. Carolinasmex.com.

Owens, Tiffany. "Worth the Drive: Arizona's Best BBQ, Diners & Drive-Ins." *Highroads* (May/June 2010).

Park, Kristin. "At 60 Years, Macayo's Still Family." *Arizona Republic*, April 5, 2006.

Pitzl, Mary Jo. "Chimichanga Launched for Arizona Official State Food." AZ Central, October 16. 2011. azcentral.com.

Polson, Dorothee. "Imaginative Entrees Add to Charm of Mi Patio." *Arizona Republic*, November 30, 1984.

Rader, Jim. "Brief History of Rueben Sandwich." Miriam-Webster Inc., 2018. rolandweb.com.

Regan, Margaret. "The Chapters of El Charro." *Edible Baja Arizona*, January/February 2017.

Saloman, Sharon. "Ocotillo Restaurant: A Story of 4 Founders." *Edible Phoenix*, December 1, 2018.

Santa Cruz, Nicole. "Tortillas to Write Home About: Hometown USA: Tucson." *Los Angeles Times*, October 10, 2010.

Simpson, Corky. "Garagiola Open's Biggest Hit with Fans." *Tucson Citizen*, January 13, 1997.

Skinner, M. Scott. "What's Hot in Safford." *Arizona Daily Star*, September 19, 2010.

Slater, Steph. "La Paloma: History, Tradition of Good Food Changes Hands." *Eastern Arizona Courier*, January 3. 2007.

Southwest Folklife Alliance. University of Arizona, May 29, 2014. southwestfolklife.org.

Sparks, Colleen. "Valle Luna Restaurant Marks 20 Years in Chandler." *East Valley Tribune*, December 12, 2017.

Stanley, John. "Founder of Macayo's Dies." *Arizona Republic*, September 12, 1999.

Stern, Jane, and Michael Stern. *500 Things to Eat Before It's Too Late and the Very Best Place to Eat Them.* N.p.: Rux Martin, Houghton, Mifflin, Harcourt, June 2009.

Swift, Carey. "A Taste of History at Macayo's." AZ Central, August 26, 2016. azcentral.com.

Tombstone Web: Tombstone, Arizona Information. "History." Tombstoneweb.com/history.

Trulsson, Nora Burba. "Chimichanga Mysteries." *Sunset*, October 1999.

Tucson Citizen. Romano Cedillos obituary. September 20, 2003.

Valle Luna Mexican Restaurants. valleluna.com.

Vincent on Camelback. https://vincentsoncamelback.com.

Vinyard, Valerie. "Mi Nidito Celebrates 65 Years in Business." *BizTucson* (Summer 2017).

Von Meter, Eric. "USS *Tucson* to Carry El Charro Fare Under the Sea." *Inside Tucson Business*, April 10–16, 1995.

Weil, Elizabeth. "Who Really Invented the Reuban?" *Saveur*, September 6, 2016.

Wikipedia. "Bracero Program." https://en.wikipedia.org/wiki/Bracero_program.

Wisdom's Café. wisdomscafe.com.

World's Greatest Cheese Resource. Cheese.com.

Wright, Suzanne. "A Dash of Wisdom." *Edible Baja Arizona*, March/April 2015.

INDEX

L

M

N

P

R

S

T

V

W

ABOUT THE AUTHOR

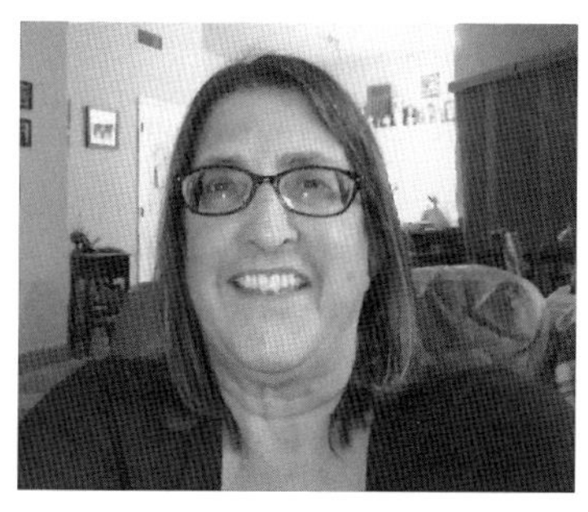

Arizona Chimichangas is the third book Rita Connelly has written for The History Press. Her previous books, *Lost Restaurants of Tucson* and *Historic Restaurants of Tucson*, were so much fun to write that when she was asked to take on the subject of chimis, she jumped at it.

Connelly first moved to Tucson in 1972 from her home state of Wisconsin and while she moved back to the frozen north a few times she came to her senses and moved to Tucson with her husband, John, and daughter, Riene, permanently in 1987. It was then that she began her writing career in earnest and soon was writing food-related articles for several publications.

Connelly was the restaurant reviewer for the *Tucson Weekly* for ten years. Her other works include articles for *Highroads*, *Experiencing Sedona*, Visit Tucson, gayot.com, sallysplace.com and other national and local magazines. Her blog, *The Well-Fed Foodie*, can be found at wordpress.com and Facebook.

She can't say which chimichanga was her favorite; instead, she encourages others to travel the beautiful state of Arizona to discover the many flavors of the Grand Canyon State.